Aspects of Modern Sociology

SOCIAL PROCESSES

GENERAL EDITORS

John Barron Mays
Eleanor Rathbone Professor of Sociology
University of Liverpool

Maurice Craft
Professor of Education
University of Nottingham

ASPECTS OF MODERN SOCIOLOGY

General Editors

John Barron Mays Professor of Sociology, University of Liverpool
Maurice Craft Professor of Education, University of Nottingham

This Longman library of texts in modern sociology consists of three Series, and includes the following titles:

THE SOCIAL STRUCTURE OF MODERN BRITAIN

The family
Mary Farmer
University of Liverpool

The political structure
Grace Jones
King Alfred's College,
Winchester

Population
Prof. R. K. Kelsall
University of Sheffield

Education
Ronald King
University of Exeter

The welfare state
Prof. David Marsh
University of Nottingham

Crime and its treatment
Prof. John Barron Mays
University of Liverpool

Patterns of urban life
Prof. R. E. Pahl
University of Kent

The working class
Kenneth Roberts
University of Liverpool

The middle class
John Raynor
The Open University
and
Roger King
Huddersfield Polytechnic

Leisure
Kenneth Roberts
University of Liverpool

Adolescence
Cyril Smith
Social Science Research Council

The mass media
Peter Golding
University of Leicester

The legal structure
Michael Freeman
University of London

Rural life
Gwyn Jones
University of Reading

Religious institutions
Joan Brothers
University of London

Mental illness
Bernard Ineichen
University of Bristol

Forthcoming titles will include:

Minority groups
Eric Butterworth
University of York

The economic structure
Prof. Cedric Sandford
University of Bath

SOCIAL PROCESSES

Bureaucracy
Dennis Warwick
University of Leeds

Social control
C. Ken Watkins
University of Leeds

Communication
Prof. Denis McQuail
University of Amsterdam

Stratification
Prof. R. K. Kelsall
University of Sheffield
and
H. Kelsall

Industrialism
Barry Turner
University of Exeter

Social change
Anthony Smith
University of Reading

Socialisation
Graham White
University of Liverpool

Social conflict
Prof. John Rex
University of Warwick

Forthcoming titles will include:

Migration
Prof. J. A. Jackson
University of Dublin

SOCIAL RESEARCH

The limitations of social research
Prof. M. D. Shipman
University of Warwick

Social Research Design
Prof. E. Krausz
University of Newcastle
and *S. H. Miller*
City University

Sources of official data
Kathleen Pickett
University of Liverpool

History of social research methods
Gary Easthope
University of East Anglia

Deciphering data
Jonathan Silvey
University of Nottingham

The philosophy of social research
John Hughes
University of Lancaster

Forthcoming titles will include:

Data collection in context
Stephen Ackroyd
and
John Hughes
University of Lancaster

Social Conflict

a conceptual and theoretical analysis

JOHN REX B.A., Ph.D.
Professor, and Director of the
S.S.R.C. Research Unit on Ethnic Relations
University of Aston

Longman London and New York

Longman Group Limited,
Longman House,
Burnt Mill, Harlow, Essex, UK

*Published in the United States of America
by Longman Inc., New York*

© Longman Group Limited 1981

First published 1981

British Library Cataloguing In Publication Data

Rex, John
    Social conflict. — (Aspects of modern sociology:
    social processes).
    1. Social conflict
    I. Title   II. Series
    301.6'3'01   HM136   80-41443

    ISBN 0 582 48123 6

Printed in Singapore by Four Strong Printing Co

CONTENTS

EDITORS' PREFACE

The first series in Longman's *Aspects of Modern Sociology* library was concerned with the social structure of modern Britain, and was intended for students following professional and other courses in universities, polytechnics, colleges of education and elsewhere in further and higher education, as well as for those members of a wider public wishing to pursue an interest in the nature and structure of British society.

A further series set out to examine the history, aims, techniques and limitations of social research; and this third series is concerned with a number of fundamental social processes. The presentation in each case is basically analytical, but each title will also seek to embody a particular viewpoint. It is hoped that these very relevant introductory texts will also prove to be of interest to a wider, lay readership as well as to students in higher education.

John Barron Mays
Maurice Craft

FOREWORD

This book revives what should be one of the most central themes in sociology. Some would say that it should be *the* central theme. Surprisingly, however, it is a theme which was lost in university sociology departments after the turbulence of the late 1960s. One might have thought that the atmosphere of those times would have led precisely to a rethinking of social and political issues in terms of conflict theory. That this did not happen was due to the fact that so many of the conflicts which aroused the passions of students and junior staff were internal to the campus itself, and that when they sought to revise sociological theory in order to deal with other problems, they turned to deterministic theories about the functioning of the various state apparatuses which were as fatalistic as the functionalism of the 1950s. The problem for sociology, therefore, is how to revive the notions of conflict and change in sociological theory without relapsing into utopianism. If this text helps to restart that argument it will have performed a useful function.

During the period of writing I have moved from a teaching department much influenced by contemporary trends in theory, to the direction of a research unit concerned with one of the most conflict-ridden areas of social life today. I should like especially to thank my former colleagues, Peter Ratcliffe, Ivan Oliver and Margaret Archer for the friendship and support which they always gave me at Warwick, and all of my new colleagues in the Research Unit for Ethnic Relations, especially Susan Bishton, Robin Ward and Malcolm Cross for helping me to produce a new and creative environment for sociological thought and research.

For the second time I have to thank Olive Heaton, whose remarkable capacity to type from my manuscript has made the production of a typescript possible, and Norma Burd and Christine Dunn who have interrupted the other routines of their office to see that all of the business surrounding the production of a book was accomplished smoothly.

For the first time I am dedicating a book solely to my wife Margaret. She has had to put up with a lot from sociology and has survived with integrity. It is good to say publicly how very much I owe to her.

John Rex

BY THE SAME AUTHOR

For Margaret

1

THE MICRO-SOCIOLOGY
OF CONFLICT

Social relations, integration and conflict

Sociology is not about unambiguous 'things'. The most elementary units which it claims to study are social relations. What, however, is a social relation? Should the term be confined to interpersonal situations marked by harmony and co-operation or should it be used more inclusively to cover all cases in which two actors respond to one another's behaviour whether co-operatively or not?

One major tradition in sociological theory, culminating above all in the work of Talcott Parsons,[1] concentrates its attention on situations of co-operation or what Parsons calls 'institutionalisation of role expectations'. As he puts it in his own terms:

the institutionalisation of a set of role-expectations and of corresponding sanctions is clearly a matter of degree. The degree is a function of two sets of variables; on the one hand those affecting the actual sharedness of the value-orientation patterns, on the other those determining the motivational orientation or commitment to the fulfilment of the relevant expectations. As we shall see a variety of factors can affect the degree of this institutionalisation through each of these channels. The polar antithesis of full institutionalisation is, however, anomie, the absence of structured complementarity of the interaction process or what is the same thing, the complete breakdown of normative order in both senses. This is, however, a limiting concept which is never descriptive of a concrete social system. Just as there are degrees of institutionalisation so there are degrees of anomie. The one is the obverse of the other.[2]

Parsons' *The Social System* and all his subsequent work which depends upon it deals with what is necessary to ensure 'shared value orientations' and 'the fulfilment of role expectations'. Thus he leaves out any sustained discussion of the 'obverse' case. It would seem, therefore, that there is a need for Parsons' theory to be complemented by a theory of those cases in which 'value-patterns' are not shared and expectations not fulfilled. Indeed, on Parsons' own admission, actual cases fall somewhere between two extremes. A theory which applies to empirical reality there-fore must be twofold, drawing upon the systematic conceptual development of two ideal types, though we need not agree to lump all cases at the non-co-operative pole under the essentially misleading term 'anomie'.

The question of conflict arises for Parsons because his is a sociological theory based upon the concept of 'action'. Thus he assumes that the ultimate theoretical entities used in his sociological explanation are 'actors' who have 'goals' in the pur-suit of which they used 'means' guided by certain 'norms'. This was spelled out systematically in his earlier work *The Structure of Social Action* and in his collaborative work *Toward a General Theory of Action*.[3]

Methodological individualism and its alternatives

Not all sociological theories do make this assumption and it has been usual, following Popper, to denote the theories which do as 'methodologically individualist'. Defining this term, Popper writes, 'the task of social theory is to construct and to analyse our sociological models carefully in descriptive or nominalist terms, that is to say, in terms of individuals, of their attitudes, expectations, relations, etc. – a postulate which may be called "methodological individualism" '.[4]

It will be noticed that Popper does *not* say that historical events are made up purely and simply of the 'attitudes, expecta-tions, relations, etc.' of actual empirical individuals. What he says is that the terms which we use referring to groups actually refer to 'models' of what goes on in the world and that these models may be analysed into more ultimate theoretical elements, viz. individual actors. These actors are theoretical entities which are the equivalent of the atoms of physical theory.

Similarly Max Weber, whose approach to sociological theory is followed here, writes that:

for the subjective interpretation of action in sociological work these collectivities (i.e. states, associations, business corporations, foundations) must be treated as solely the resultants and modes of organisation of the particular acts of individual persons, since these alone can be treated as agents in a course of subjectively understandable action.[5]

But he also insists that what is important for sociological interpretation is neither the action of a particular concrete empirical individual nor a statistically average individual, but rather an ideal or theoretical type.[6]

According to Weber's definition of sociology the subject deals with 'the interpretative understanding of social action' and social action is social 'insofar as its subjective meaning takes account of the behaviour of others and is thereby oriented in its course'.[7] Hence the term 'conflict' which is our concern here refers to action which is 'oriented intentionally to carrying out the actor's will against the resistance of the other party or parties'.[8]

The non-sociologist will recognise the standpoint of methodological individualism as in accordance with our common-sense understanding of social relations and social facts and may ask why this should be a matter of debate at all. It is important to point out, therefore, that not all social theory bases itself upon the concept of action. Durkheim, for example, appeared to point in a different direction with his injunction that social facts must be treated as things[9] and this concept has come to play an increasingly important part in sociology. Neither the 'structuralism' of Levi-Strauss and its Marxist counterparts, nor what appears to be its opposite, ethnomethodology, are concerned to analyse the social order in terms of action. Thus there is a large body of literature in contemporary sociology which has no place for the concept of 'conflict' as Weber uses it. In the structuralist tradition especially, emphasis tends to be placed on a different concept, namely that of 'contradiction' between system parts.[10]

The 'double contingency' of social relations

We shall here follow Parsons as an action theorist and with him will recognise the central fact about social relations, that they are, as he says, 'doubly-contingent'. We shall, however, unlike

Parsons, explore more fully what is involved in this double contingency.

When we speak of social relations being doubly-contingent we mean that their existence depends not merely on what one actor expects but upon what another actor does in response to those expectations as he perceives them. There is, however, a wide range of possibilities involved in the relationship between these contingencies which must be distinguished in a theory of conflict.

Parsons' concept of the 'institutionalisation of role expectations' assumes what he calls 'a twofold structure of binding in' of the process of interaction. Put simply, what he suggests here is that it must be assumed that what one actor (whom he calls 'Alter') does will be affected by the fact that either he has a need for the other actor's (called 'Ego') action for its own sake or that he needs Ego's approval for affective reasons and that he shares with Ego the need to conform to a standard.[11]

The first distinction which needs to be made here is between instrumental and affective action. Clearly, it may not always be the case that Alter requires Ego's approval. Much action and particularly that which is involved in conflict is no way dependent upon affective ties. The existence of such ties does complicate matters, but the complication itself can be best understood if we first deal with the simple case of instrumental action, where Alter has no affective need for Ego's approval and is purely concerned to respond to his action.

On the question of conformity to a standard as one of the aspects of 'binding-in' of a social relation, Parsons appears to have two things in mind. One is the normative control of ends, for he sees sociology as being unlike economics and utilitarian thought, in which ends are thought of as random, and as being based upon some notion of a community of ends.[12] The other is that, whatever the end, the means which may be employed and hence, the actions which are regarded as permissible are subject to normative control. From the point of view of the theory appropriate to the study of conflict neither of these limitations of subject-matter can be accepted. We must take into our purview both situations in which ends are random from the point of view of our analysis and situations in which there is no limit to the means which may be employed.

The contingencies of social interaction

In the basic situation of interaction which is our starting point we assume two actors, whom, for convenience, following Parsons,[13] we shall refer to as Ego and Alter. Each of these we assume to have ends of his own. We assume that Ego seeks to communicate his expectations of Alter's action to Alter, that Alter may or may not fully receive this communication, that he may or may not feel obliged to limit his action according to normative standards and that he may or may not comply with Ego's expectation.

The communication of expectation

The first 'contingency' involved in this interaction then concerns the communication of expectations. It seems clear that this communication will not always be perfect or complete. Thus it is always possible that before Alter begins to consider his response to Ego's expectations he may be unclear about or misunderstand what those expectations are. One of the possible meanings of 'anomie', the term which Parsons uses as the polar opposite of institutionalisation, refers to such misunderstandings. It is important, however, to separate it from the other contingencies which we shall discuss below. This is particularly true if we consider what is called 'conflict resolution'. The practice of conflict resolution often and quite rightly lays emphasis upon misunderstanding, since strikes and wars, for example, may result from such misunderstanding. But it is equally true that the whole of conflict does not arise from this source, and to lump all the possible reasons for non-co-operation or non-compliance under the heading of 'anomie' is unhelpful and misleading.

Normative standards

The next issue with which we have to deal concerns that of normative standards, both those governing ends and those governing means. Alter clearly may or may not feel that his conduct should be governed by such standards. Quite commonly what happens is that Ego makes appeal to such standards as a reason for Alter's compliance, but Alter may reject the standard independently of his decision whether or not to comply.

Deviance

Nor does the matter end there. If it did we should quite happily be able to include the theory of deviance under the theory of conflict. But there is at least a prima facie case to be made that some kinds of deviance have as their main characteristic the fact that, even though Alter accepts the standards as applying to him, he disobeys them. This is a central point made by Parsons in his analysis of the genesis of deviance from a psychoanalytic point of view and also by some other deviance theorists such as Matza, who sees deviants not so much breaking rules as stretching them to accommodate deviant behaviour within the rule.[14]

True conflict

If, however, we suppose that all of these issues are cleared out of the way, the possibility of conflict still remains. Alter may have fully understood what is expected of him, but rejects the line of conduct which Ego requires and be prepared to pursue both his own goals and the line of action by which he proposes to achieve them. It may be argued, indeed, that it is this issue and this issue alone which is the appropriate concern of the theory of conflict.

The profiles of social action

All in all, however, it would seem that actual social action may be thought of as falling between two types. On the one hand there is the Parsonian institutionalised case in which there is an agreement over legitimate ends and of norms governing appropriate means for the attainment of ends, in which Ego fully and completely communicates his expectations, and in which Alter, apprised of this information, does what is expected of him both out of a desire to sustain Ego's approval of him and because the action required is both normatively and instrumentally satisfying to him. At the other extreme (the situation of full and absurd anomie) there is no community of ends or normative consensus about appropriate means, in which, in so far as Ego attempts to communicate his expectations he is unsuccessful, in which Alter, having some more or less confused understanding of those expectations, finds that he cannot accept the demands made upon him, is not motivated to comply and hence pursues some (to Ego) unacceptable line of conduct.

Each of these elements of course varies independently and the actual point along any line of variation will differ from case to case. Thus any particular line of social action must be located for each variable at its appropriate point and in theory a profile for each action may be worked out, as in Fig. 1.

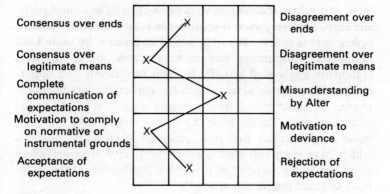

Consensus over ends			Disagreement over ends
Consensus over legitimate means			Disagreement over legitimate means
Complete communication of expectations			Misunderstanding by Alter
Motivation to comply on normative or instrumental grounds			Motivation to deviance
Acceptance of expectations			Rejection of expectations

Fig. 1

This is how any action might be placed between the pure Parsonian type and its opposite. Taking a narrow view, the theory of conflict would deal basically with the last line in Fig. 1 only and would aim to predict the way in which interaction would develop once conflict had become apparent. In a wider sense, however, the theory would have to deal with consequential interaction in each of the cases of disturbance of the Parsonian ideal type. It is this latter alternative which will be accepted in the following paragraphs.

The dynamics of conflict situations

Normative disagreement

Where there is a normative disagreement over ends or means regarded as legitimate, there are two possibilities. In the limiting case which would exist in a state of war or in the case of contact between individuals from two totally different cultures between whom there had been no communication, there would be no possibility of anything but open conflict. In most cases, however, some discursive resolution of the disagreement over values and norms might follow. This would take the form of an appeal by the parties to higher order values and norms which they might share, and even in the case of two totally strange cultures some moral discourse might occur in which the parties made their own values and normative systems clear to one another. In any case, however, such discourse need not necessarily lead to agreement. Conflicts are rarely settled in practice by some kind of medieval disputation and in many cases appeal to moral arguments might well actually be used expediently and opportunistically to justify action which the parties actually intend to pursue in fulfilment of their interests regardless of the moral issues involved. On the other hand, one should note the point made by Habermas that it is precisely when social relations which have been sustained through inequality of power break down that the possibility of discursive justification of the moral basis of social interaction arises.[15]

Some distinction might be made here between disagreement over ends and values on the one hand and disagreement over appropriate means. The more severe the conflict the more likely it is that questions of ultimate ends and values will be raised. Smelser[16] has made the point that in situations of psychological strain there is a tendency to move to more and more radical definitions of the disagreement. According to his analysis the party who is threatened moves from a diagnosis based upon lack of means available, to one of personal blame, to one concerned with norms, and, finally, to one which raises questions of ultimate value. This analysis assumes that some measure of personality disturbance is involved and that the diagnoses are themselves irrational, but there is no reason why in cases where the parties are not subject to strain, and may be thought of as acting in a cool and collected way, discursive argument might not proceed from lower to higher levels.

Communication of expectations

The notion that 'conflict' is due to misunderstanding is one which looms large in the theory of conflict resolution. Mediators in industrial and international disputes frequently diagnose conflicts as due to misunderstanding and seek to clarify not only the moral orientations of the parties but their actual expectations of one another which are assumed to have been misunderstood. There is often substance in this belief and the mediator might well be able to show that the practical meaning of words used by one party is not the same as the meaning understood by the other. Ethnomethodology has been particularly useful to sociology in drawing attention to the way in which quite simple terms and sentences take for granted whole realms of meaning. It also suggests that in social encounters new definitions of social reality are continuously being negotiated.[17] Naturally, too, one should recognise that in these definitions cognitive and evaluative elements cannot be totally distinguished. On the other hand, and possibly contradictory to the ethnomethodological emphasis upon the irremediable embeddedness of particular statements in wide and open-ended meaning contexts, it should be noted that, when discussions arise about the meaning of expectations in a relationship, what might actually be negotiated is precisely a cutting off of the particular statement of expectations so that its diffuse overtones are explicitly excluded.

Motivation to comply

Turning to the question of motivation to comply, the first thing which we have to notice is that compliance or non-compliance with a norm which Parsons emphasises is only one case amongst several. Normative sanctions, as both Weber[18] and Etzioni[19] suggest, may coexist with or be less important than coercive or utilitarian ones. That is to say the individual may comply because of a balance of power which he perceives in the situation or because it is in his interest, particularly his pecuniary interest, to do so. In these cases Ego, faced with Alter's non-compliance, would be likely to increase the severity of coercive sanctions or 'pay more' in accordance with the state of the market. Such developments obviously overlap with the analysis of true conflict, but it is important that they be mentioned here as one of the sources of *motivation* to comply.

Man's relationship to norms may vary from that which occurs when the individual is so completely socialised that, on the level of his personality system, he actually needs to do that which he is required to do, to a situation in which he accepts the normative order as a part of his environment. Parsons[20] has shown how, in Durkheim's work, there is a movement from the latter definition of the influence of the social on the individual to the former, though he himself employs a socialisation model in *The Social System*.[21]

In the intermediate grey area it is especially worth noting the case in which the normative and the power order are combined. Weber,[22] for example, speaks of a subjective belief in the minds of actors that authority is legitimate. This belief may be more or less strong, ranging from total moral commitment to obedience to a general acceptance of the legitimacy of authority with only a more or less mechanical obedience to commands.

Parsons, in his development of his socialisation model, does not, however, it should be noted, assume that socialisation is an unequivocal process. He believes that in certain ideal learning situations socialisation may be complete, but his account of the genesis of deviance in *The Social System* makes it clear that socialisation may well engender strain and ambivalence on the part of the 'socializee'. Characteristically he argues this ambivalence involves both a desire to retain the approval of the socialiser and a desire to aggress against him. This ambivalence is resolved by doing one of the two things doubly hard in order to repress the other. Such 'compulsive' behaviour may be generalised from the particular interaction to all interactions in the relationship and from the troublesome relationship to others. The individual thus becomes psychologically committed to deviance.

We should certainly agree that this psychological dimension arising from disturbances in the personality system is a feature of many cases of deviance and may well affect otherwise pure conflict situations. Parsons also draws our attention to the fact that the focus of the deviance may be either against persons or against norms as such, the latter case being particularly relevant under the present heading. While we may wish to emphasise rational conflict ourselves, it is perhaps worth noticing that deviance theory has probably recoiled too much from psychoanalytic type theories, and that Merton's famous essay[23] is often misunderstood as following this trend, whereas it can only really be understood if one recognises that his various types of deviant should be thought of as having developed a generalised personality disturbance.

Compliance with norms or the development of shared value-orientations, then, is by no means the simple unequivocal element in social relations which Parsons' early chapter in *The Social System* suggested. Even in his own account the socialisation may lead to deviance and resistance. What we now need to assert, however, is that even though Parsons' account has considerable explanatory value, it explains neither the whole of deviance, nor the wider aspects of conflict which may be entirely rational, involving no element of strain at all.

True conflict situations

Ideological argument

We must now turn to what must be the core of conflict theory. To arrive at this we assume that Alter fully understands Ego's goals and his own, that he has properly understood Ego's role-expectations, that he has his own understanding of the norms which act as game-rules in his interaction, that he is not psychologically disturbed about his relations with Ego or with the normative order, but none the less consciously pursues ends through lines of action which conflict with Ego's expectations.

The pursuit of Alter's ends in conflict with Ego's expectations will essentially involve the mobilisation of sanctions against Ego, just as Ego, his expectations having been frustrated, may be expected to mobilise sanctions to ensure Alter's compliance. In the ultimate type of conflict Ego and Alter might try to deal with the problem radically by destroying each other or using physical violence to alter each other's expectations and conduct, but before this situation is reached it is likely that alternative ways might be found of modifying these.

How soon after the parties, having diagnosed their situation as one of conflict, resort to the most drastic sanctions of all will not be solely dependent upon factors internal to the interactive system or social system which their relationship constitutes. As Parsons points out[24] *social* systems interact with and are affected by the processes of the cultural system and the personality system. Thus cultures vary in the readiness with which they permit or encourage parties to a conflict to resort to violence. The notion of rational law as a basis for ordering social relations is at least a very important myth in Western European civilisation, as Weber has pointed out,[25] and it is also the case in industrial relations in the liberal democracies that some kind of quasi-legal institutions operate to regulate disputes before they go on, even to the use of limited sanctions such as the strike and the lockout. In the so-called 'developing societies' there may well be an absence of such myths and institutions during the process of industrialisation. It is obviously also true that the resort to more drastic sanctions might follow more readily in the event of personality disturbances on the part of the parties, such personality disturbances being likely to lead to direct attacks on the other party or on the norms which he proposes, or upon a compulsive avoidance of any conflict for fear of the violence which might be unleashed. Psychological factors of this kind are always deeply involved in conflicts of a more intimate kind, e.g. marital conflict.

Where there are limitations on the immediate resort to conflict and where there is no particular psychological basis for the conflict, the first stage in the pursuit of that conflict will take the form of moral or legalistic argument. If, however, there is a real conflict of ends, the purpose of the argument on the part of the parties to it will not be simply to arrive at *the* moral truth, but rather at that interpretation of the relevant morality which allows for the attainment of each party's goals. It will consist in special pleading and rationalisation by each party on his own behalf coupled with an attempt to expose the dishonest or ideological nature of the other's position. It is interesting to notice that the latter aspect of moral and political conflict has been the basis for the development of both the psychology and sociology of ideology. Mannheim, as is well known, faced up to the full consequences of this situation by drawing attention to the fact that the charges of ideology brought by one party against another could also be directed against his own case.[26] But the point which he makes about political conflict can be generalised. There is an opportunistic aspect to moral argument

in simple personal conflict and the whole matter is institutionalised in normal courts of justice which are organised on the basis
of arguments between adversaries.

The next tactic which the parties to a conflict may pursue is
concerned not so much with the moral as with the cognitive
aspects of their situation. As we have seen, one of the variable
elements in any social relation is the degree to which 'Ego's'
expectations are successfully communicated. It may also be the
case that disputes disappear when these are clarified and sheer
misunderstandings are eliminated. When there is real conflict,
however, the parties to that conflict may well be concerned to
'confuse the issue' by representing their expectations falsely.
This is particularly true on the part of those who have power
and/or are proposing to exploit the other party, and very often
false mediation of the dispute might be suggested, which has as
its objective, not the reconciliation of interests, but the suppression of the conflict through obfuscation. Thus when Alter is told
that there is really no conflict but only misunderstanding, this
may be only a tactical ploy designed to prevent his pursuing his
interests or goals. Naturally enough the same tactics will be
employed by the other side, which will also seek to employ its
own false mediators.

Little further need be said here about the role of the normative system relating to means which may be used here, beyond
what has already been said about negotiation about ends and
values, except that this normative system may be resorted to
opportunistically as a means of advancing the parties' separate
interests. It is not surprising that deviance theory has explained
deviance in all ways ranging from absolute moral theories
through cultural and psychological ones to those which are based
purely upon the notion of conflict. All such theories have relevance to different types of academic discourse, but the theories
which are relevant to the pursuit of conflict are those which
emphasise the labelling of the conduct of the other as deviant
and those which emphasise the essentially rational and conflictual nature of deviance.[27] Ego in our basic scheme, of course,
always seeks to obfuscate the issue by reference to absolute
moral values or by 'psychoanalysing' his deviant partner. Alter
resorts to labelling theory and the new radical criminology. The

question, however, is not whether one is right or wrong but that both types of theory may be used to advance interests.

The more drastic sanctions

It is obvious, then, that the first stages of conflict will be basically verbal and ideological and conflict may terminate when one party imposes his moral or cognitive definitions of the situation on the other or where possibly they agree that they have made mistakes. Many conflicts in fact are settled in this way, and settled with more or less 'justice', taking 'justice' to refer here to a situation in which the two parties are not misled into accepting a settlement which prevents their attaining their goals. We must now turn, however, to the use of sanctions of a more drastic and non-ideological sort.

More drastic sanctions involve both those of a passive and an active sort. The principal passive types are those of passive resistance and working to rule, both of which deny co-operation to Ego by Alter.

Passive resistance involves quite simply the denial of any normative basis for Ego's demands. Alter tells Ego that although he may not ultimately withhold his co-operation, he will give it only if it is made clear that he does so because force is used against him. By so doing, of course, he renders less effective the relationship which Ego is trying to set up. Ego is now faced with a situation in which the cost of achieving his objectives is increased not merely in terms of the outlay on weapons, police, prisons, etc. but in terms of the fact that it becomes clear that each action has to be forced out of Alter. It could be the case that for long periods Alter remains inactive during a period of punishment and only after that does what is required of him, and in the extreme case Alter might even be prepared to die rather than conform. Implicitly, too, Alter may be appealing to third parties thought of as upholders of some moral order which Ego's expectations are thought to have infringed, thus directing the argument back to the moral realm.

We should, of course, qualify the assertion in the previous paragraph to the effect that reliance on force is more costly to Ego than reliance on moral persuasion. The 'ideological apparatus' necessary to sustain moral compliance may be more costly in some cases where absolute power exists. This is usually the case with slavery. Passive resistance works best as a way of forcing Ego to alter his demands only where this ideological apparatus already exists and does not have to be specially set up. In these circumstances it is powerful because the cost of violence is additional to the outlay on ideology.

Even in cases where the ideological apparatus exists, however, the cost of strengthening it to meet an emergency may be greater than the cost of resort to violence. It could indeed be the case that the limitation on this resort to violence and, hence, the possibility of effective passive resistance is confined to relatively few societies in which there are well-established supreme legal institutions (as for example in the United States) and also a humane culture which appreciates that resort to violence is unusual. Frantz Fanon was once challenged by pacifists whose experience of the Civil Rights Movement in the United States led them to argue that similar methods could have been used effectively in Algeria. He argued that such methods had been tried, but that the French colonialists had no compunction about resorting to force.[28]

'Working to rule' is another tactic which Alter might employ which is close to passive resistance. In part this has already been discussed in so far as it implies a wilful unwillingness on the part of Alter to understand the full meaning of Ego's expectations or of the normative order within which interaction occurs. But it must be raised again here because it is a way of increasing Ego's necessary outlay on the 'ideological apparatus' to make his meaning clear and/or because, by allowing Alter to convert himself into an automaton, it proposes a system of total detailed supervision of his every act.

In what has been said in the past few paragraphs, the implicit reference has been to interaction of a political kind between members of different collectivities. Similar points might be made, however, about small-scale interpersonal interaction, as in marriage. The principal difference appears to lie in the fact that in the former case Alter opens up the need for violence or force as an alternative to a normative order, in the latter case such a possibility is opened up as an alternative to personal affective interdependence. A spouse who resorts to passive resistance or a work to rule is essentially drawing attention to the fact that the relationship is no longer 'bound-in', to use Parsons' term, by love.

The more active forms of resistance by Alter take the form of denying Ego facilities or services, withdrawing from or changing the nature of the relationship, preparing to use force against Ego or destroying him physically. Each of these courses of action may be undertaken by Alter himself or by Alter in conjunction with allies.

The denial of facilities and services may take several forms. In the first place Alter might realise that Ego relies upon him for facilities and services other than those now demanded and may withhold their provision in order to put pressure on Ego to withdraw his present demands. The threat of such action is implicit in the bargaining that goes on in any multiplex relationship. Secondly, Alter might withhold gratuitous extras which he has been accustomed to providing within the relationship presently in question, as for example when teachers withhold additional extra-contractual duties such as playground supervision in furtherance of a wages dispute. Thirdly, the individual might simply refuse compliance himself across the full range of what is now required. Finally, he may not merely do this, but take steps to ensure that no one else offers the services.

This last type of action, organising a strike, is of course one of the best-known and most common forms of peaceful conflict in advanced industrial societies. It is paralleled by a lock-out of the workers by the employers. Both actions are effective in so far as the vital interests of the other party are affected. A totally effective strike would be possible only in so far as no other source of profits was available and profits were the *raison d'être* of the employer's existence. A totally effective lock-out would be dependent upon the denial of subsistence to the workers.

In fact the strike and the lock-out do not usually have these drastic consequences, and social security on the one hand, and legal limitation on industrial action on the other, ensure that what happens in the dispute is really only the mobilisation of relatively restricted sanctions which can be weighed in terms of their cost against the cost of yielding to the other side.

Again, it should be noted that the elements which are

involved in the interaction between members of large-scale collectivities have their parallel in small-scale interpersonal situations. In the first place it is quite possible for the parties to relationships of this kind to deny facilities to one another as a way of
bringing pressure on one another. But, perhaps more impor-
tantly, when what is sought is a flow of affective rewards, some
or all of these may be denied. Although less basic than the
means of subsistence which an employer may deny to his workers, they may perhaps be thought of as an essential need for
which such relationships provide. It is also possible to think of
the affective rewards available in secondary groups and in mass
society as the equivalent of social security in this respect, which
prevents 'starvation' in the event of a 'lock-out'.

The next alternative available consists of the more radical
steps of withdrawal from the relationship altogether or its total
reconstruction on a new basis. Withdrawal, of course, depends
in essential matters on the possibility of going elsewhere to
obtain equivalent facilities or rewards. This is a normal part of
the operation of the market mechanism in industrial societies.
The object of withdrawal in this case will be to increase the price
which the buyer is willing to pay or the service or facility which
the seller is willing to provide. It may, however, be of a more
complete kind intended to make the partner in the relationship
suffer or to put an end to that kind of relationship altogether.
Such intentions would appear to make withdrawal a preparatory
phase of a reconstruction of the social relationship or 'revolution'.

Revolutionary restructuring of a relationship is conditional,
however, on there being no alternative supplier. Societies may
lose members through emigration, but gain others through
immigration. Employers may lose dissatisfied workers, but be
able to recruit in other labour markets. A deserted or divorced
spouse may find a new partner and remarry. Thus, unless the
separating partner in any of these relationships is able to restrict
the availability of substitutes who can take his place withdrawal
will not alter the nature of the relationship which he has left.

Whether or not one of the parties withdraws from a relationship, another possible way of responding to an unsatisfactory
situation will be to try totally to reconstruct the basis of the

relationship. This may be done by a skilful process of bargaining over the terms on which facilities are offered so that gradually the balance of power between the parties is altered, but in the more radical cases other kinds of power, including violence, may be deployed in order to bring about such a change.

There is a long-standing debate in sociology about whether power is to be conceived of as a resource of a social system or whether it is to be thought of in zero-sum terms so that the more one party has the less another has.[29] This argument, however, is not strictly relevant here. Certainly, so long as a social relationship remains stable, power, usually kept very much in the background, is a resource providing a sanction for the various sorts of demands made upon individuals. But, in a conflict situation which develops to the point which we are discussing here, one of the parties sees power as being controlled by the other to his own disadvantage and seeks to check its use by the other, take over its control or use new sources of power against it.

A struggle for power may have a number of outcomes. A settlement may be achieved when the cost of engaging in the struggle beyond a certain point appears greater than any gain which might be achieved. Such a settlement would be backed by relocated centres of power which backed the new terms of the relationship. An alteration of these terms would, by the same token, be a sufficient basis for ending the power struggle. Another possibility, however, is the more revolutionary one in which the aggrieved party, having gained what he was originally seeking, might see the possibility of further gains and go on to demand wholly new terms.

When we speak of power here we are referring not simply to physical violence but to a whole range of means whereby one party compels another to obey his will. But the exercise of physical violence is undoubtedly the ultimate sanction along a scale of drasticness of means used. In a normal situation there is a specialised institution, viz. the state, which has a theoretical monopoly of the means of physical violence. It may, it is true, permit some degree of violence amongst its citizens in the course of their disputes, but it has the ultimate say in how much individual violence there may be and exactly when and where. The move to the use of violence in areas where it has not normally been allowed by the state is therefore drastic, not only in the sense that physical violence is regarded with horror as compared with other sorts of persuasion in and of itself, but because the use of such violence is in effect an act against the state.

Small boys, when they fight, often recognise that the fight will end when one can bear the pain inflicted on him no more and makes some kind of act of submission. Similarly, in the use of violence in other social relationships the aim is to achieve submission. But how far one might go in the use of violence in order to obtain an act of submission remains open to question. In the most extreme case the individual using violence will be willing to kill if necessary, and the threat of being killed and not merely injured will certainly enter into the decision whether or not to submit in more cases than those in which killing is likely.

In the most ultimate case one party does actually kill the other. In this case he challenges the state's monopoly of legitimate physical violence and will either himself be removed from the process of interaction through incarceration or execution, or he will alter the nature of the state itself by establishing his own right to use violence. In these circumstances the ultimate basis of law and order will have broken down and, albeit on a small scale, a state of civil war will exist. Of course, in so far as the 'enemy' has been killed, this state of war will have led to victory. Of more importance is the case in which 'the enemy' consists of not one but a number of persons, and the question which then arises is how much killing the enemy can stand and how much he can himself inflict. This case, however, is one to which we can return only after we have discussed the more complex problems involved when the parties to a conflict are groups or collectivities.

The case of the 'victorious revolution'

More to the point immediately is the question of what happens when an individual 'Alter' wins total submission from 'Ego'. As we have seen above, a power struggle often issues in some sort of compromise in which Alter and Ego both modify their goals and their actions and accept new agreed norms after they have decided that there is less to be gained by continuing the struggle. In these cases a new normative order is established which has additional strength because it rests upon a balance of power which has been put to the test. But in the case of total victory and submission Alter will either find that he is simply liberated from a relationship which was both irrelevant to his needs and oppressive, or he must put Ego to work on his own behalf or he must find new role-partners.

At the moment of total victory and submission the incipient new relationship rests solely upon acquiescence by those who submit on the basis of the realities of the power situation. Such a situation, however, quickly begins to change to one which is more normatively structured. In the first place the very need of the defeated to keep out of trouble leads to the development of a kind of normative control. Then this relatively calculating attitude is reinforced by habit. But beyond this there occur those processes which Parsons refers to as the twofold binding-in of the social relation. Those who have submitted and are now, for the purpose of the analysis, the new Alters must be socialised into accepting the new norms and of wanting the new Ego's approval.

The basis of the new relationship will involve on the one hand fixed patterns of behaviour on the part of Alter which do not have to be demanded by Ego because Alter comes to do them because he thinks that they are right, and other more flexible patterns which have to be demanded by Ego and which therefore depend upon Alter's attitude towards him.

So far as adherence to norms is concerned there is surprisingly little said in the literature of sociological theory about how this comes about. W. G. Sumner suggests that in the first place there arise shared group habits or folkways and that, when these are challenged by exposure to alternative patterns, they tend to take on a moral quality.[30] Durkheim tells us that those ways of behaving are learnt in the context of intense collective activity. According to him moral actions are socially induced and any such action 'gets its efficacy from the intensity of the mental state in which it is placed. It is this intensity which creates what we call moral ascendancy.'[31] For Freud, morality depends upon the attachment to any transgression of a required form of behaviour of a sense of guilt which is explained by an original sexual interaction with the parents. G. H. Mead[32] speaks of the development in the child of the concept of a 'generalised other' to which he feels obligated. For Weber[33] it seems that beyond coercion and utilitarian sanctions, the binding together of a society depends upon a subjective belief in the minds of those who obey that the authority exercised over them is legitimate.

Of these writers only Durkheim and Freud explain rather than describe how men come to adhere to moral norms. The Durkheimian explanation is unconvincing because in differentiated societies there are no collective ceremonies of all-embracing kinds which he finds in the Aboriginal corroboree. Mass behaviour, it is true, does hold some sway over the individual, but it is generally recognised that such behaviour has a kind of irrationality about it which distinguishes it from the genuinely moral. In general terms, without accepting the whole Freudian account of the Oedipus concept in detail, we may say that the Freudian account of the origins of morality is more convincing. All individuals emerge from the family with some conception of right or wrong and the acts which they are called upon to perform, if they are to be regarded as moral, must be judged in terms of these standards.

The limitation of a Freudian account of moral obligation, however, for our purposes lies in the fact that it gives no account of the way in which morality is culturally developed, generalised and rationalised. Mead's concept of the 'generalised other' may be seen as important here in suggesting that the basis of obligation shifts as children develop socially and intellectually. Weber, in one of his types of legitimate authority, viz. the rational–legal type, suggests that in Western civilisation at least the specific and detailed obligations learnt as a part of small-scale civilisation become rationalised and systematised into codes.

What all this suggests is that we may think of the interactive situation which our newly victorious Ego inherits as one in which, quite apart from the question of Alter's interests or his affective relation with Ego, he must reckon on Alter as having some more or less systematically rationalised commitment to norms. This means that he will be able to construct a more efficient, less costly system of interaction with Alter if he can demonstrate that his demands accord with those norms. This will be no less true if his appeal to these norms is cynical and self-interested and takes the form of casuistry.

The second aspect of the binding in of Alter's and Ego's conduct will lie in the sphere of interpersonal and affective interaction. Parsons' account of this interaction belongs essentially in the psychoanalytic tradition and sees it as a recapitulation, albeit in a more developed form, of patterns of interaction learned in infancy. The individual will learn required patterns of behaviour in so far as there are in the learning situation adequate discipline, adequate security, adequate rewards and adequate permissiveness. That is to say, Ego must be clear and explicit in his demands, he must retain the trust of Alter, he must reward him for conformity and he must let him have scope to 'let off steam' during the frustrating period of learning new patterns.

Weber's two types of legitimate authority other than the rational–legal one are also relevant here. Men will obey for reasons of tradition or for the opposite reason that someone who breaks with tradition has unusual or 'charismatic' qualities. In our model, Ego would probably try to get the best of both worlds: (a) by emphasising the continuity of his demands with what went before; and (b) using his charismatic appeal to justify change. Such personal ties would serve to reinforce rational–legal authority even when such rational–legal authority has primacy.

Taking the Parsonian and the Weberian accounts together we might say that Ego has to establish that Alter has positive affective attitudes of love or respect towards him and that Alter also accepts his right to exercise authority. Such personal ties will serve to reinforce commitment to new norms and make more effective the new relationship which was established originally on the basis of a power struggle.

The completed circle of social conflict

By the time our new Ego has established this new regime the social process will have gone full circle. Our account of social conflict showed how, when the binding in of a social relationship by normative controls and personal ties was broken down, pure conflict emerged. We have now shown how, when a new regime is established, these bonds are restored. This cycle will occur even when the intervening conflict is of a highly disruptive kind. We should note here, however, that the process whereby Alter displaces Ego and becomes Ego is one which faces the greatest difficulty. Where conflict and power struggle leads to a compromise, norms will not have to be so radically altered, and both norms and affective relations will be strengthened by the fact that they have relative continuity and yet reflect the actual balance of power.

The psychological dimensions of conflict

We have sought, so far as we could, in this account, to exclude from our analysis the psychological dimension of conflict. That we were not able to do so completely is evident in our discussion of strain leading to the shift of conflicts about norms to the level of more ultimate values and in our discussion of the psychological dimensions of deviance. We should now note, however, that psychological aspects of conflict are systematically related to social ones.

In a polar limiting case two parties to a social conflict may engage in the conflict without the conflict becoming personal or affective at all. Skilled politicians and industrial negotiators sometimes achieve this degree of calculating detachment, making only a pretence of hostility to the other party to deceive him and to encourage their own supporters. It is possible that in so far as they do they fight or negotiate more successfully. But few human beings in institutional contexts are able to eliminate 'personal feelings' entirely.

What happens on the psychological level when conflict is pursued is well described by Parsons in his chapter on deviant behaviour and the mechanisms of social control.[34] According to his account the essence of the psychological process is to be found in the adjustive and defence mechanisms which come into operation in Alter's personality when Ego varies his expectations. He becomes ambivalent in his attitude both to Ego himself and to the norms. Ambivalence means that he retains a 'cathexis' (a desire) for Ego and a commitment to the norms. But this cathexis and commitment can no longer be undisturbed. He also wants to break with Ego and with the normative system. He may live out this ambivalence and have his cake and eat it by allowing now one side of his ambivalence, now the other, to be expressed in segregated contexts or on segregated occasions, but where this is not possible he will be driven to repress 'one side of the ambivalent structure so that only the other side receives overt expression'. 'If it is the negative side which is repressed, ego will be attached to alter and/or be motivated to conform with the normative pattern in question. If the positive side is repressed, conversely ego will tend to abandon his attachment to alter, in the sense of giving it overt expression and to refuse to conform with the normative pattern.' (Note that Parsons is looking at this from the point of view of the deviant and therefore calls him 'ego' whereas we have started from the point of view of 'society', and call the potential deviant 'Alter').

It is characteristic of whatever line of conduct our Alter pursues that it will be 'compulsive', i.e. pursued somewhat rigidly and with double the strength. But this has its consequences. Alter is now making extra demands on Ego and he is also liable to personality disturbance. In the example which Parsons gives, Ego has demanded what Alter regards as unduly high standards in a piece of work. Alter reacts to this with resentment which he represses and becomes compulsively anxious to secure Ego's approval. His demand for approval, however, is of double strength so that 'the same level of approval which would have sufficed before is no longer sufficient'. Ego then 'goes critical' or starts acting in terms of defence and adjustment mechanisms. So the conflict escalates unless there is some intervention to arrest it, basically by someone reassuring the parties, allowing for the letting off of steam and *not* reciprocating the unwonted behaviour.

If, however, there is no intervention to arrest this process, not merely will it be the case that the particular conflict will escalate, but the disturbed individuals which it produces will behave compulsively and rigidly in other situations. This is, of course, particularly true if the original interaction giving rise to the disturbance occurs during the first five years of life or, according to Parsons, during the years of adolescence. Thus the capacity of individuals to handle conflict rationally in the way which we have suggested above is limited and this psychological dimension of conflict will be superimposed upon and distort the patterns which we have outlined.

No doubt Parsons' account of these troubles draws upon a particular line of theorising in the psychoanalytic tradition and should not be taken as the last word in these matters. None the less there is surprisingly little in the social psychological literature which deals with the psychological aspects of *interaction*. Moreover, it is interesting that Merton's[35] attempt to account for the structured origins of deviance actually makes many psychological assumptions and that his account of types of deviance is actually very close to Parsons'.[36]

What we would wish to emphasise in this chapter is that conflict does have both sociological and psychological dimensions. It would obviously be absurd to deny, as many politically orientated writers do, that conflict is simply a rational political process and that the attempt to study its psychological dimensions is purely ideological. But it is also important that theorists of conflict resolution of a psychoanalytic orientation should not represent conflict as only having psychological roots. Such work would indeed be ideological.

Our micro-sociological model should indeed provide the basis for an applied social science of conflict. It might not be a science of conflict resolution only, because the truth is that some conflicts cannot be resolved. Nor should it pretend to be a science which only points to open and honest behaviour, for the materials are here which would show how to resolve or end conflict by deceiving one of the partners. But here, as elsewhere, the theory of social science can be used by good and bad men alike and social scientists as such have no right to dictate what is morally or politically right. All they can do is to indicate what is involved in a particular conflict situation including what would be involved in ending it, resolving it or promoting it.

So far we have dealt with situations of a dyadic type. That is to say our basic model has been one of an interaction between two parties. We now have to turn to the theory of multi-person structures and of those situations in which the parties to a conflict are not individuals but collectivities. Central to this discussion will be a sociological analysis of the concepts of a market and of class and class struggle.

2

CONFLICT AND MARKET SITUATIONS

Dyadic and multi-person structures

The analysis of dyadic social interaction which formed the substance of our first chapter owes much to Georg Simmel[1] and there is no doubt that he is the founding father of the study of social conflict.[2] He also wrote explicitly on the subject of conflict and on the implications of a money economy. None the less Simmel wrote discursively as though he were lecturing, with many *ad hoc* asides and with a tendency to depart from his initial focus on the structure of interaction in the direction of psychological and cultural generalisations of a somewhat loose kind. When he moves beyond the study of the dyad or two-person relationship he tends to be diverted into asides on the nature of extra-marital affairs or to the general psychological influence of numbers on the individual social participant. Again he reflects discursively on the ambivalence involved in the integrative and dissociative aspects of conflict without sharpening up his conceptual analysis along the lines suggested in the previous chapter. Finally, although he wrote about the implications of a money economy[3] he does not adequately conceptualise the complex structural nature of market behaviour.

In order to proceed further it will be necessary to proceed more thoroughly with an analysis of multi-person structures of social action. These include markets which are closely related to, and always liable to break down into, conflict and groups and quasi-groups which often constitute the parties to conflict. In this chapter we shall be especially concerned with markets.

Market Structures

A market is a complex form of structured interaction which includes bargaining, exchange and competition. It also leads, when its pure form gives way to collective bargaining, to group formation, and groups generated by one market may merge in greater or less degree with groups generated in others. These latter processes are essential to the understanding of class formation and class conflict which is a major theme of Chapter 4.

The evolution of economic exchange

Clearly, the process of economic exchange is a central one in modern society. In the liberal–utilitarian–individualist Utopia such exchange relationships should encompass the whole of social structure. They are thought to be essential to the most prized of liberal values, individual freedom. They differ from relationships of status on the one hand, which restrict the freedom of the individual, and from pure conflict relations on the other, which are not thought of – as are exchange relations – as bringing equal benefits to the two parties.

Economic exchange, however, is not a natural feature of the human social condition. It is possible to extend the use of the term to include non-economic exchange, emphasising the reciprocity of social action as writers from Malinowski[4] to Blau[5] have done, but, where two parties have fixed customary duties to one another, even though they may be reciprocal, they do not necessarily imply the rational–calculating orientation of one party to the behaviour of the other which is of the essence of exchange.

The fulfilment of human needs in the simplest societies follows from the performance of duties by one man or woman to another which are, as it were, written into particular roles. Thus amongst the Trobriand islanders the mere fact that a man is brother to a woman means that he has duties to his sister which ensure her subsistence, while she and her children have complex reciprocal duties to him. The social structure, the system of rights and duties, is written into the kinship system. Hence, to describe the kinship system is to a very large extent sufficient to describe the social structure.

Sir Henry Maine[6] and Herbert Spencer,[7] who followed him, would have described such relationships involving fixed duties as relationships of status to be contrasted with the relationships of contract which form the structure of modern societies. Malinowski, however, who was always intent on rendering comprehensible the apparently irrational behaviour of savages, departed from this conception of status relations in his interpretation of Trobriand behaviour in three ways. He suggested that all relationships in simple societies were governed by the principle of reciprocity. He drew attention to a complex form of ritual trading known as the 'kula' which serves to establish interpersonal bonds beyond the range of the kinship system.[8] And he suggested that there was also an incipient form of bargaining over the exchange of goods along with these other forms which foretold our own type of market behaviour.[9]

Of particular interest here is Malinowski's account of the kula exchange. 'Trading' relationships here were not the same as, and stretched beyond the bounds of, kinship relations, but they were by no means simply relations of barter such as speculative bourgeois economic history suggested. Compared with market exchange in advanced industrial and commercial societies they had certain obviously irrational features. The objects exchanged were not treated as commodities and their value lay in their ritual significance and in their individual history in previous acts of exchange. Reciprocity was evident, it is true, in that each gift required a counter-gift, but this by itself by no means implies an equivalence with economic exchange.

In fact some of the simplest forms of exchange have almost opposite qualities to those of economic exchange in the market. Whereas market transactions involve trying to get as much as possible for as little as possible, it is often a feature of exchange in primitive societies that the parties try to outdo each other in their generosity. This reaches its ultimate extreme in the custom of potlatching amongst the Indians of North-west America amongst whom one exchange partner seeks to aggrandise himself against his partner by the generosity of his gift.[10] There are also many oddities in the use of simple forms of money which show that pure economic ideas have not been allowed to break out of the shell of custom and status.[11]

It is against this background that economic bargaining appears problematic. Despite Malinowski's suggestion in *Crime and Custom in Savage Society* that in the exchange of vegetables for fish there is a 'mental chalking up' when gifts of vegetables and counter-gifts of fish are offered, the notion of giving the minimum to get the maximum is not a natural form of behaviour and depends upon a prolonged process of cultural evolution. Benjamin Nelson's work, *The Idea of Usury – From Tribal Brotherhood to Universal Otherhood*, describes how the group within which brotherhood prevails grows progressively smaller as the surrounding world of market relations increases in importance.[12]

Malinowski's 'mental chalking up' is a new and revolutionary principle in human affairs. But, as he describes it, it is still a matter for normative control. One chalks up what is due, but what is due is a matter of a shared concept of value and justice. No similar concept affects the higgling of the market in which the two parties are individualistically orientated, each trying to give as little as possible for as much as possible. In so far as a normative order governs such relations it rests solely upon the outlawing of fraud and force, as Parsons in his gloss on Durkheim's *Division of Labour* makes clear.[13]

This moral limitation on exchange relationships does of course make a difference and one which is crucial in distinguishing exchange and conflict. Exchange cannot exist where the rule is:

The mountain sheep are sweeter, but the valley sheep are fatter.
We therefore deemed it meeter to carry off the latter.

If there can be resort to force of this kind there is likely to be conflict but there can be no point in exchange.

Exchange in economic theory and sociology

The study of peaceful bargaining and exchange appears at first to be the central theme of economics and it might be thought that any theory of the sociology of economic exchange must involve reference to the debate amongst economists about the theory of value. Indeed it might seem that we should take sides in the debate between the theorists of marginal utility and the tradition, which continues strongly amongst European sociologists at least, which is based upon the labour theory.

In fact, however, our purpose is different from that of the economists who, above all, are concerned to provide a theory of the movement of prices. We are concerned with the development of a theory of social interaction and of a particular kind of social interaction which falls somewhere between normatively ordered co-operation and outright conflict.

The economics of marginal utility is regarded by some as a theory which refers to an ideal relationship in which, Marxian and like theories notwithstanding, no element of compulsion and no sanctions operate, other than the free choice of the parties in terms of their own scale of values. If, however, this were what was meant all we could say was that this was a limiting case equivalent to, although different from, Parsons' completely institutionalised relation.

Such a relationship would, of course, be of some interest in itself. It is important to note that, along with the Parsonian case in which the ends of Ego and Alter are normatively structured and co-ordinated, there was another case in which Ego and Alter have a multiplicity of ends, each of them being capable of being realised in greater or less degree, but involving some concept of scarcity so that Ego and Alter both have to choose and to economise, not realising all their ends, but simply realistically maximising their utility. Clearly, at least in Western capitalist culture, relationships of this latter kind are a theoretical possibility.

Looking more closely at this matter, however, it becomes clear that what the economic theorists are talking about is an abstraction in which this kind of economising action is divorced from its institutionalised context and the sole area of interaction is a totally free market. In such a theory there is no scope for any constraint on choice resulting from property and power and no interference with the market through any kind of monopoly.

Marx and Weber both saw that the kind of economising action and bargaining which we have been discussing operated as a main structuring element in society only in limited historical circumstances. Marx was particularly concerned with the labour market where, given the capacity of labour power to produce more than its own cost of reproduction, it was possible, through the denial of the means of production to the workers, to compel them to enter into acts of unequal exchange which yielded a surplus to the capitalist. From this he went on to argue for the historical uniqueness of the system and its long-term instability. His observations on this are of relevance even if we have doubts about his commitment to the labour theory of value, because clearly it is the case that the relationship between an ideal–typical employer and an ideal–typical worker is not simply a free economising one of the type suggested in the theory of marginal utility.

Weber, on the other hand, while accepting the theory of marginal utility in general terms, sees that all actual bargaining and exchange relationships are constrained by power and the distribution of property. Thus he writes (significantly in his chapter on 'Political communities'):

It is the most elemental economic fact that the way in which the disposition over material property is distributed among a plurality of people, meeting competitively in the market place for the purpose of exchange, itself creates specific life-chances. The mode of distribution, in accord with the law of marginal utility, excludes the non-wealthy from competition for highly valued goods; it favours the owners and, in fact, gives them a monopoly to acquire such goods. Other things being equal, the mode of distribution monopolises the opportunities for profitable deals for all those who, provided with goods do not necessarily have to exchange them. It increases, at least generally, their power in the price struggle with those who, being propertyless, have nothing to offer but their labour or the resulting products and are compelled to offer their products to subsist at all. The mode of distribution gives to the propertied a monopoly on the possibility of transferring property from the sphere of the use of 'wealth' to the sphere of 'capital', that is, it gives them an entrepreneurial function and all chances to share directly or indirectly in returns on capital. All this holds true within the area in which pure market conditions prevail. 'Property' and 'lack of property' are therefore the basic categories of all class situations. It does not matter whether the two categories become effective in the competitive struggles of the consumers or producers.[14]

What Weber is doing here, despite what are actually confusing references to 'competition' and 'classes' is to develop a theory of bargaining which rests upon a notion of the distribution of property and power. He dismisses the idea of the classical economists that land, labour, capital and entrepreneurship are natural factors of production, each naturally receiving its own reward and, with Marx, agrees that the rewards of capital and the functions of entrepreneurship result from the advantage accruing to the propertied in the labour market because of their possession of property. The basis of Weber's theory lies, therefore, not in the market-place but in political institutions within which the market-place is located.

Bargaining situations

The distribution of property gives rise to a number of what Weber, following Marx and some of the economists, calls classes or, more exactly, class situations. We might say 'bargaining situations'. There are, however, as many class situations as there are types of property. Thus

class situations are differentiated; on the one hand according to the kind of property that is usable for returns; and on the other hand, according to the services that can be offered in the market. Ownership of dwellings; workshops; warehouses; stores; agriculturally usable land in large or small landholdings – a quantitive difference with possibly qualitative consequences; ownership of mines; cattle; men (slaves); disposition over mobile instruments of production, or capital goods of all sorts, especially money or objects that can easily be exchanged for money; disposition over products of one's own labours or of others' labour differing according to their various distances from consumability; disposition over transferrable monopolies of any kind – all these distinctions differentiate the class situations of the propertied just as does the meaning which they can give to the use of property, especially to property which has money equivalence.[15]

Thus capitalist societies, but other types of society too, are property structured and provide for unequal bargaining. Such relations may well break out into open conflict in changed political circumstances when the right to property is challenged. In so far as they are not, they are likely to be organised by the powerful in terms of the twofold Parsonian process of binding-in. A propertied Ego will seek to establish affective ties with the less propertied Alter and persuade him to accept that his forced behaviour is actually in accordance with norms. The Marxian demystification of economics represents it as an attempt to get

Alter to accept not quite this, but rather that the required behaviour is (a) to Alter's advantage, and (b) according to the natural order of things.

Competition and market situations

All that Weber says in the quotations above applies to hypothetical pairs of economically interacting actors who offer each other, or demand and are forced to give, services and goods. Strictly speaking they do not involve competition, but only bargaining and exchange. We move towards the more complex notion of a market when we add to this bargaining additional actors on both sides of the exchange and competition between them. In order to understand this we shall have to consider what is involved in the social form of competition and its relation to that of conflict.

The essence of competition is that two actors are seeking the same goal, whereas in the case of conflict, as we have outlined it, they are seeking different and contradictory goals. But, in so far as, in the case of competition, the negative aspect of Ego's or Alter's orientation is emphasised and his aim is construed as stopping Alter from attaining the mutually desired end which is in scarce supply, competition may be construed as a 'special case of conflict'.

Competition may take place for any end that is in scarce supply. It may also be more or less naked. The intensity of the competition will depend upon the degree of scarcity. In some cases there will be no question of sharing the gains. Either Ego achieves his objectives to the exclusion of all potential Alters or he fails to do so. In some other cases of lesser scarcity Alter may simply obtain a smaller portion of what is available, or as in a race for a prize 'come second'. In this case the consolation of a share, albeit a lesser one, or of second prize, will serve to abate the severity of the conflict. It is also possible that Ego will combine with some Alters but not others to agree to share to the exclusion of the others whatever is available according to some formula.

Competition, like bargaining, may be more or less bound by norms. At one extreme is the case of naked competition in which

Ego will do anything to deprive Alter and to attain his own ends, including injuring him or killing him. At the other is the case in which only certain actions are deemed to be legitimate as in a game which is subject to rules. In between these cases are cases in which there are overall limitations on what actions the parties might take, deriving from taboos and prohibitions, generalised ethics and from the legal framework. Thus killing and injuring the other party may be outlawed, certain forms of action may be regarded in terms of a shared ethical code as cheating and there may be restrictions on the advertisement of one's product or the denigration of that of one's opponent.

A particular case of competition to which the last example implicitly refers is that of competition for resources in a market. The parties to the competition may both be seeking suppliers, and in pursuit of this aim be offering goods or services in exchange. In this case the main tactic employed will be to offer these goods or services at a lower cost than one's competitors. Obviously, however, such a tactic is a two-edged sword. There are gains but there are also costs. In the first place at least, command of supply will depend upon being able to produce at a lower cost than competitors, though it may be worth while to bear a relatively high cost oneself in the knowledge that a more or less permanent relation with the supplier may be established for a flow of supplies, while the other party is forced to abandon the struggle because even the temporary interruption of his supply 'puts him out of business'. In general the capacity to win in a struggle for market bargains will depend upon the ability to bear costs and this in turn will depend both on the property he possesses (both generalised wealth and the command of specific resources) and on his organisational capacity.

Competition for scarce bargains differs from simple cases of conflict in that it involves at least three parties, the competitors on the one hand and the exchange partner on the other. Structurally, therefore, it actually differs from dyadic conflict. In such dyadic conflict the outcome may be the negotiation of new terms with the interacting partner or his elimination and the search for new partners. In competition for scarce bargains, however, the basic relationship with the supplier may continue even after competitors have been eliminated or 'put out of business', though this relationship with the supplier now becomes a dyadic one, in which bargaining and economising may give way to conflict.

So far we have used the rather awkward term 'competition for scarce bargains' to describe a case where there is a plurality of competitors on one side of the exchange process and basically only one individual 'supplier' on the other. This, however, is not, of itself, a true market situation. A market situation exists only where there is a plurality of 'buyers' seeking to make advantageous bargains with a plurality of 'suppliers' subject to the condition that both buyers and suppliers compete with one another. Thus we do not have a true market situation when bargaining occurs or competition occurs each in isolation from the other. Nor do we have it unless there is competition on both sides prior to the striking of bargains.

We have seen with Max Weber how any bargaining situation is affected and made unequal by the disposition of property and other resources. But even if these are assumed to be equal, new sanctions enter into the market situation which affect what bargains are struck and with whom. It is the possibility of the use of these sanctions and the attempt to eliminate them which makes the bargaining situation inherently unstable.

The sanctions of bargaining in a free market

The basic sanction affecting bargaining in the market is the threat to go to another supplier or to seek new exchange partners. This is a sanction of a kind not discussed in our previous chapter and it is one sufficiently powerful to make other sanctions less necessary. Furthermore, it involves freedom of choice and the peaceful pursuit of goals, and this is why the liberal–utilitarian Utopia of a market-based society seems to be a credible alternative to all other ways of attaining a multiplicity of goals.

On the other hand the use of this sanction works for both parties to the bargain in a free market. If only one party could employ it he would be in a position to force down the price to the lowest level compatible with a continuing supply and this indeed is what happens in situations of monopoly amongst buyers. (In the case of a suppliers monopoly of course the price will be as high as possible.) When both sides are subject to competition the situation reverts to what it would be as between individual buyers and sellers. Prices offered on both sides are forced down to their lowest level and the agreed price is fixed in a bargain between the remaining two exchange partners determined either in terms of marginal utility or in terms of extra-market power or in terms of both.

Restrictions on the free market

The natural tendency in such a free market situation is to eliminate the possibility of using the sanction of going to an alternative buyer. As Adam Smith was the first to note, employers were first to do this in the labour market. They conspired together to force down the wages of workers, through an agreement not to pay above a certain level. In these circumstances inevitably the workers also conspired together not to work for less than a certain level of wages. Similar phenomena occur in the markets which are generated between buyers and sellers in all the various economic transactions to which Weber refers.

From market process to collective bargaining and conflict

Total monopoly on both sides of any market eliminates the market process as such. What we have instead is collective bargaining, and collective bargaining must rest upon sanctions other than market ones since these have been eliminated. We are therefore back to the sociology of bargaining or of conflict. The processes which are set in train will be those which we discussed in our previous chapter, though when they arise out of an original market situation they will take specific forms such as the strike, the lock-out and the boycott, and the actors, instead of being individuals, will be collectivities or organised groups.

The level of drasticness of sanctions which occurs in these cases is in the first place the intermediate one of denying to the other the facilities or services which he seeks. As bargaining proceeds, however, the conflict may develop in one of two alternative directions. On the one hand both parties will seek to contain it and reduce its drasticness by appealing to norms. On the other the conflict may escalate to include a wider denial of facilities or the use of actual physical violence.

Collective bargaining and the role of 'rational' argument

The first of these alternatives is the one pursued in the case of labour disputes by the experts on industrial relations who are employed by both sides as well as by governments anxious that the possibility of escalation should be avoided. These interventions may involve appeal to economics, to normative systems which are claimed as relevant and ultimately to authorities who are thought to stand for the 'national interest' rather than the interests of the parties.

So far as the appeal to economics is concerned this may involve something of a myth. If in fact the bargaining relation in question rests upon collective bargaining fully developed there can be no question of some economic proof of the appropriate terms for settlement. In such cases what is happening is that either one of the parties is trying to cover a settlement which is in his own interest with an appeal to economic science, or perhaps that both parties are doing so to avoid having to face up to the fact that they are actually engaged in a power struggle. The real basis of a settlement would then be based upon an implicit recognition of the balance of power and the economic arguments simply used to find a formula which accorded with this basis.

It might be, however, that the appeal to economics refers not to the terms which are being negotiated in the situation in question but to the costs which the parties have to meet in other markets within which they have to obtain other supplies to stay in business. Only in the case in which all markets have been transcended by an overall collective bargaining situation so that all negotiations were in fact between the same two sides would this be a myth. In capitalist societies workers' representatives may see this as the long-term outcome of collective bargaining and political action, but realistically they have to admit that such a final stage of class confrontation has not been reached and that they and their employers are constrained by external market forces.

The second area of argument to be deployed involves explicit appeal to norms. Such norms may have real significance for two reasons. On the one hand they may be the result of past negotiations and have been jointly sponsored by the parties now in dispute. On the other they may represent 'custom and practice' between two parties who have for a long time been engaged in collective bargaining and in the co-operative activity which results when truces are struck. Appeals of this kind may be used opportunistically and new glosses placed upon old shared meanings and it is obvious that as the balance of power shifts attempts will be made to replace old norms with new ones reflecting the new balance. Again, however, it must be admitted that in situations of sustained economic interaction and collective bargaining the parties might well find that they can appeal to a shared normative structure.

Where there are norms of this kind which have been brought into being by collective negotiation it is unlikely that any appeal to norms or laws of a more general kind will be effective. Precisely because there are norms which have been specifically sponsored by the parties as relevant to their condition, other norms which do not have this backing will be treated with suspicion. Equally, an attempt to impose legal obligations in place of those which have been collectively negotiated is not likely to succeed without the suppression by government of the collective bargaining process itself.[16]

This brings us to the question of appeals to the national interest. These can have little relevance to a situation in which 'the nation' is committed to a free market economy. Such a commitment implies that the best course in the national interest is to let bargaining continue, and it is contradictory to suggest that in order to achieve this any particular process of bargaining should cease. But in most capitalist societies there is some kind of central regulation of the economy and some degree of planning. The parties to a conflict will be persuaded to modify their actions in accordance with this national interest therefore, in so far as they can be convinced that it is realistically in accordance with their interests (e.g. if restraining inflation yields better real returns than pressing a wage claim to the full) or if there is an affective patriotic identification with the state more powerful than economic self-interest. Undoubtedly, however, this is the type of appeal which may be opportunistically and ideologically used by one of the parties rather than constituting a normative basis for settlement.

The extension of the market model to non-economic situations

In the previous paragraphs we have referred, by way of illustration, to the case of employer–employee bargaining over wages and conditions and in thinking of most European capitalist societies it is appropriate that we should do so, since empirically this type of bargaining constitutes a main axis on which politics are structured. But we should recognise that the principles which we have been outlining are general structural principles applying to all those bargaining situations set up as a result of the differentiated distribution of property and power which Weber calls class situations. It might well be the case, moreover, that in countries like the USA, where trade unions are less powerful and market negotiations and collective bargaining are more diverse and complex in character.

The nature of collective bargaining skill

All the factors we have referred to serve to suppress or modify collective bargaining rather than being of its essence. Collective bargaining itself requires skill and capacities, and the outcome of the process might well depend on how well the two sides mobilise these skills and capacities. In an earlier work referring to the action of subordinate working-class groups the present author wrote:

the factors involved in the power situation of the dominated group are highly variable factors such as the strength of their aspirations, their capacity for corporate action, their numbers, and the degree to which their social role vis-à-vis their rulers becomes indispensable. The strength of the aspirations of such a group will depend upon the effectiveness of indoctrination and the quality of leadership, upon the intensity of their exploitation and upon the example of similar groups in other societies. Their capacity for corporate action will again depend upon leadership and organisational ability as well as on the organisational examples coming from outside the group, including the example of the ruling class.

The other factors are ones which are continually changing because of advances in technology. Technological changes produce new roles in the social system, give a greater strategic importance to some old roles or increase the number of people in particular situations. This has been true not only with regard to the social institutions connected with production but in other spheres also, for instance in the field of mass communications and in that of military organisations.[17]

On the question of organisation it might now be added that the capacity of a group generated as a collective bargaining group in a market situation might be affected by the existence of alternative forms of social bonding. A collective bargaining group is, after all, an artificial grouping of individuals, and ethnic, religious, cultural and kinship ties are of a more primordial kind. Of course, if the collective grouping coincides, as it sometimes does, with one of these then it will enjoy additional strength in the struggle. But where it does not, artificial *Gesellschaft*-type relations must be established in the face of communal *Gemeinschaft* ties and thus is probably only possible in a society in which cultural conditioning has produced habits of individualism. Even then there are differences of organisational style ranging from spontaneously emerging groups to groups in which members make a virtually whole-time commitment. The creation of such groups of dedicated members was a particular achievement of Lenin in his concept of the 'Vanguard party'.[18]

Clearly, too, another factor which affects the outcome of collective bargaining struggles is leadership. This includes two elements. On the one hand there is negotiating skill. On the other there are the charismatic qualities of the leader which are important in holding the group together and thereby increasing its power. The pressures on a leader are complex. There will be pressure on him to routinise the process of settlement which would turn him into an executive of the collective will of the negotiators taken collectively rather than as an agent of his members. He will, in any case, have to 'deliver the goods' even if he achieves tough rather than soft settlements. Yet he must not lose communication with the feelings and interests of his members. Moreover, in the negotiating process, he will have to develop appropriate skills as to the precise timing of revelations of the power at his command. Some negotiators will be able to simply say 'no' as their most effective tactic. Others will be skilled at making the least costly concessions at the right time in return for concessions from the other side.

The more drastic sanctions

Behind these factors which come under the headings of mobilisation and negotiating skill lie the factors which form the real substance of collective bargaining. These concern the pressures that can be brought to bear through the denial cf control of facilities and services.

The main issue here is what sanctions are regarded as legally admissible in the particular negotiating context. In an industrial dispute, for example, the right to withdraw labour might be accompanied by more or less stringent controls on picketing, and picketing may itself take more or less drastic forms. Again the picketing of the gates to stop workers going into a factory may be accompanied to greater or less degree by actions of solidarity, including secondary picketing to stop the employer getting supplies and secondary boycotts to stop him selling his products. Moreover, the industrial action may be pursued at one extreme in such a way that third parties are not hurt or at the other with a view of hurting the general public and thereby compelling their support. Inevitably, too, developments in this area lead to propaganda by both parties about who is responsible for any injury to the public.

At the margins, enforcement action, even in the most routine disputes, raises the question of the sanctions which may be employed both to enforce compliance by the other side and to maintain solidarity amongst one's own side. The situation being an unstable one, there is likely to be recourse to some measure of violence. A central question then is at what point in the escalation of conflict is violence permitted or banned.

Generally speaking, in capitalist societies a high value is placed upon the peaceful settlement of disputes. Because certain forms of collective action are permitted, it is argued, resort to violence is unnecessary. It may be the case, however, that settlements resulting from the use of violence are more advantageous than those which exclude it, and it may also be the case that one of the parties to the dispute, seeing the state as upholding, through its monopoly of the means of legitimate physical coercion, a flow of disadvantageous settlements, may seek to challenge and modify the state's monopoly. In these cases in greater or less degree the situation of collective bargaining moves towards one of civil war based upon conflicting economic interests. This is a topic to which we shall return when we discuss more explicitly the Marxist theory of class conflict.

Again we have used the example of industrial relations to illustrate general points. In doing so we do not exclude the possibility that class conflicts may occur, as Weber suggested, between parties other than capitalist employers and workers. In theory such conflicts may occur and have the same potential for escalation along a gradient of drasticness of sanctions at any point where economic exchange occurs and an entrepreneur may be seen as entering into such relations with all those who contribute factors of production – with those who provide capital, raw materials and facilities of all kinds, as well as with customers. Generally speaking, however, the resort to more drastic sanctions is taken only by those who are less able to use the enforcement capacities of the state on their own behalf. In a capitalist society, even if we do not represent the state as an executive committee controlling the affairs of the bourgeoisie, it is usually the case that employees and wage-earners as such have less access to the enforcement agencies and are more likely to take matters into their own hands, whereas the existing patterns of enforcement and the ideal of peaceful settlement of disputes suits the interests of those placed in other positions by the property system well enough.

Affective and symbolic elements in collective bargaining

In all that we have been saying we have assumed rational and non-affective action on the part of the parties. But here, as in the case of individual interaction, individuals whose expectations are frustrated are likely to become disturbed on the personality level. Particular frustrations of their own ends or particular demands on the part of the opposing party may well lead to a sense that trust has been broken and security threatened. In these circumstances it is unlikely that the frustrated party will either accept the new demands (the case of successful 'learning' which Parsons discusses) or simply go on coolly and rationally pursuing their ends (which Parsons does not discuss). Most likely in a collective bargaining situation these attitudes will be of those of compulsive alienation, that is to say that they will suppress their desire to win back the compliant behaviour of their opponents by going doubly hard in the direction of punishing him and of violating norms by which they had previously been bound. At the more drastic points along the gradient of means used such attitudes will lead to a further increment of violence.

Attitudes of this kind are also reinforced by symbolic expressions. Thus the history of industrial disputes has been accompanied by the development of a tradition of folksong which celebrates the heroism of figures on 'our side' and the perfidy of 'our opponents' and such a tradition always develops out of the battles of a 'civil war'. Particularly important, too, are occasions such as the funerals of martyrs. Even if a death has been quite accidental it will be represented as a martyrdom and the funeral itself might serve as an occasion of mobilisation if not actually as a new occasion of battle.

Leaders and negotiators are also likely to be affected by these attitudes and events, and they will act as countervailing factors to those which make for skilled cool-headed negotiation. On the other hand there is the possibility that a skilled leader will use the feelings of members as a mobilising factor to add strength to the negotiating position. In these circumstances symbolic occasions may be used to canalise random outraged feelings into organised effective mobilisation. Whatever settlements are achieved, however, it will be necessary to gain acceptance for them in a way which assuages outraged feelings. Roughly speaking, the negotiator and leader on these occasions has to perform the role of the social control agent in Parsons' scheme and to stop the compulsive attitudes of members from escalating beyond the point at which they usefully contribute to mobilisation.

Exchange in functionalist and conflict theory

What we have been seeking to show in this chapter so far is that economic exchange cannot be treated simply as part of the stable integrated structure of social relations. This is how it is treated too often within structural–functionalist theory which posits, on the one hand, fully institutionalised relations in Parsons' sense, but, in some areas, the permitting of the pursuit of self-interest, either because such action is private or because it is seen as leading to mutually rewarding settlements through exchange. Clearly, exchange can be mutually rewarding and reliance on the market mechanism does to a large extent provide the means of satisfaction of needs for the population at large. But exchange is also an unstable disturbing and dangerous element in the structural–functionalist Utopia. The theorisation of this aspect is an essential complement to structural–functionalist analysis.

This aspect of the importance of exchange processes has been obscured by the development of exchange theory as a special branch of sociology. What writers like Homans and Blau have done is to suggest that essentially integrative actions and relations can be better conceptualised in terms of exchange rather than in terms of some normative paradigm. Homans uses the concept to draw attention to the way in which the rewards which result from the mutual exchange of services act to condition the parties to pursuing what, from a social point of view, are desirable forms of conduct. Blau on the other hand, using more of an economist's than a psychologist's model, concentrates on exchanges of goods and services which are mutually rewarding. We need not deny either of their theses. What we suggest is that their account is incomplete and that the dynamics of the exchange process do in some cases at least lead to social conflict and social disruption. What sociology needs is a theory of exchange which does justice to both of its faces.

What we envisage is not a society that consists solely of escalating conflicts. To claim this would simply mean repeating in the opposite direction the error of the functionalist emphasis upon integration and stability. We see the market mechanism as a complex set of arrangements which sometimes works well as a means of providing utilities for its participants but which also has a potentiality for conflict. Naturally, therefore, we may also expect that in any social system which places reliance on the market there will be control mechanisms designed to contain such conflicts. Parsons, in the most generous interpretation,

may be seen not so much as positing a society built out of completely institutionalised social relations, but rather as describing
these control mechanisms. As Devereux suggests, Parsons' social
system is based upon an understanding that 'society represents a
veritable powder-keg of conflicting forces'[19] and that it is order
rather than conflict which is problematic for him. None the less
our problematic is that of conflict, and Parsons, having made his
sociological analysis of order so central to sociological understanding, it is precisely conflict which has to be explained. We
see the process of market exchange as one major source of that
conflict.

In pre-capitalist societies the market as a means of satisfying
the needs of the population was confined to limited areas of
human activity. Other matters were thought to be too sacred to
commit them to its hazards. As Marx and Engels put it in the
Communist Manifesto: 'bourgeois-capitalist society drowned the
most heavenly instances of religious fervour, of chivalrous
enthusiasm, of philistine sentimentalism in the icy waters of
egotistical calculation' and 'resolved personal worth into
exchange value and, in place of numerous indefensible chartered
freedoms, has set up that single unconscionable freedom – Free
Trade'. In fact it turned nearly every possible object of human
striving into a commodity. Even sex-love and salvation eventually came to be marketed. The wider the area of the market-
exchange system the greater was the potentiality for conflict.

Markets planning and conflict

Inevitably the irrationalities of a market system have led to
demands for its supersession by a system of planning so that the
satisfaction of important human needs is no longer dependent
upon the accidents of the interplay of market forces. Durkheim,
in his first use of the term 'anomie' spoke of the anomic division
of labour, and pointed as an alternative to the moral integration
of the various occupations;[20] Max Weber noted that the formal
rationality of Western capitalism (i.e. rationality of means) did
not imply substantive rationality,[21] (i.e. provision for the satisfaction of substantive needs). Finally, Marx saw the division of
labour as resulting in the alienation of the worker's own

labour.[22] Moreover, these analyses of the system by sociologists were backed by demands from those who actually suffered at its hands. Thus the process which Marx and Engels described in the *Manifesto* was put into reverse. The survival of capitalism itself demanded that certain basic needs of welfare should be satisfied by other than market means leading to a substantially rational provision for education, housing, health and social security. In some cases where industrial production could not be carried on for private profit it was taken over and managed by the state. And examples of new industrial societies emerged in which the whole of industry was taken into a system of bureaucratic planning.

Such developments, however, do not imply a disappearance of interest groups, nor a disappearance of conflict. Weber's formula of 'disposition over material property' covers not merely the case of outright ownership, but also that of *de facto* control, and, since in a politically and bureaucratically governed system, there are still distinctions to be made between those who control resources and those who do not, it follows, in his terms, that class situations (or what we have called bargaining situations) will continue.

We need not follow Weber here in detecting a sinister bureaucratic interest, or the dissident Yugoslav Communist, Djilas, in seeing the party *apparatchiks* as a new class.[23] Both may be correct. What we do need to notice, however, is that, since the control of the production of resources is now in the hands of a political party or political parties, conflict goes on at a political level either between individuals and the party or between parties. Access to resources now depends upon the individual's access to political power.

Resource conflict in the welfare state

In the welfare state the goods which are publicly provided are not always available in equal degree to all citizens. In the case of the publicly owned housing stock for example, there are houses of varying quality and these are made available to individuals in terms of a points system in terms of which they must qualify. The political power of different groups determines what goes into the points system and who qualifies, and those who are placed in differing positions by this system are divided in their interests, giving rise to new political groupings or what have been called housing classes.[24] Similarly, public school facilities and medicine are of unequal quality and some system has to be found of assigning services of different quality to different people.

The notion of 'housing classes' referred to above has been criticised by Colin Bell[25] on the grounds that whereas the concept of class implies an exploiter and an exploited, with the use of the concept of housing class it has not always been clear who is exploiting whom and what relational aspects are involved. A similar question might well be asked even if the term 'class' is taken to refer not to one group exploiting another but to exchange relationships leading to collective bargaining. Who, it might be asked, is negotiating or bargaining with whom?

The answer to this question is that we are not, indeed, speaking of exchange relations (or exploitative or bargaining relations) between two classes at all, but the relative position of groups of individuals within a politically and bureaucratically organised allocative system. They are, however, in competition and in conflict with one another because resources are scarce and some get better treatment than others. In this case the negotiating process (or we might say 'class struggle') takes place immediately at the political level. In the exchange, bargaining and exploitative relations we mentioned earlier, non-political sanctions were employed at first and these gradually gave way to the use of political power and violence or to the use of state power. As soon as the last alternative is used we find ourselves in the position which the housing class concept suggests, viz. where parties use their degree of leverage on the political system to advance their interests in competition with one another.

Marx, it should be noted, recognised that class conflict as it developed was bound to be political. In a famous passage, he writes:

The economic conditions have in the first place transformed the mass of the people of a country into wage-workers. The domination of capital has created for this mass of people a common situation with common interests. Thus the mass is already a class, as opposed to capital, but not yet for itself. In the struggle, of which we have only noted some phases, this mass unites, it is constituted as a class for itself. The interests which it defends are the interests of its class. *But the struggle between class and class is a political struggle* (our italics).[26]

Thus, for Marx, class struggle was ultimately political. In our discussion of the escalation of sanctions arising out of collective bargaining we also argued that the ensuing conflict was political in character. So long as the state acts in the interest of one class the struggle of other classes is a struggle against the state. When the state itself provides goods and services the struggle goes on amongst interest groups within the state.

We may indeed go further than this in our analysis of group bargaining or class struggle under the welfare state. In so far as a private sector of provision exists in such matters as housing, medicine and education there is a struggle to maintain public expenditure against private expenditure in these matters and the state may be seen as acting on behalf of groups which are disadvantaged in market situations against those who benefit from them. It is no answer to this to say that the services are in the interests of the privileged and those who have power in the market, since, even if they are, how much is conceded as a matter of bargaining and conflict? It is through political means directly and not through market bargaining or collective bargaining that the disadvantaged seek to improve their condition and the state negotiates on their behalf.

Conflict in a fully planned economy

In discussing the welfare state the situation to which we refer is one in which only some needs are satisfied through political and bureaucratic means. In a fully socialist society the actual process of industrial production is carried on by the state. But this by no means implies that bargaining between differentially placed groups disappears. The bargaining simply takes place on a political plane. This is true of negotiation about workers' wages and also about all the negotiations which a state-run enterprise must conduct with its suppliers and its customers. To some extent, indeed, when an overall socialist system of planning has been achieved there is actually a return to the market mechanism.

The reason for this return to the market mechanism is that, in its absence, conflict is likely to depend upon non-economic and particularly political sanctions. Such conflict, however, endangers the unity of the state itself. Thus the agents of the state must reassert their claim to ultimate political authority and the monopoly of the legitimate use of violence. Hence, in the Soviet Union, after a period in which independent trade unions and a degree of independence for firms were tolerated, parties as such were outlawed except for the single party which sought to unite key members of different groups and different enterprises in a unitary structure transcending in its aims the special interests of different groups.

At this stage, more completely than ever before, groups with different interests have to fight for them in political terms. The arena of struggle is within the party itself and struggles for power within the party may reflect the interests of groups differentially placed with regard to the control of resources. This could mean, and undoubtedly did under Stalinism, a situation where any expression of conflicting interests was regarded as treason and the main form of conflict was between the representatives of the state and dissidents. In these circumstances the cost of such a system became too high and the subsequent reforms led to some decentralisation of power and control over resources and the consequent toleration of economic and political bargaining processes.

Conclusion: the essentially political nature of the market

We may now sum up the main themes of this chapter. We started by defining the nature of social interaction within the market as compared with relations of co-operation on the one hand and conflict on the other. But we saw that it was in the very nature of market bargaining that it rested upon a political distribution of property and resources and that the conflicts which it generated would not necessarily be contained within the market-place. The political and sometimes violent nature of this conflict made it a threat to the state's monopoly of the means of physical coercion, and indeed the conflict was often fought out by parties within the state itself.

Bargaining and conflict over resources may thus be seen as taking a political form, even if we start from the strictly economic market-place. When, however, goods and services are provided politically and bureaucratically by the state itself then bargaining and conflict over those resources are expressed through political parties and the struggle for power, the parties trying to use their control of state power on their own behalf.

Finally, we have considered the case of a fully planned economy. Here all bargaining over rewards and resources must take place in a political forum. The pressure on the state of managing such negotiations, however, might well result in some resort to a controlled market mechanism within the plan to resolve disputes which might otherwise threaten the state itself. In the case of the Soviet Union, however, a new element enters the picture, namely that of the single party which excludes conflict and bargaining through a multiplicity of parties and also restricts conflict and collective bargaining within institutions through the disciplines of, and required loyalty to, the party which cross-cuts affiliation to interest groups of any kind.

In all of these cases we have concentrated on groups differentiated in terms of their economic interests and hence potentially liable to give rise to conflict. Exchange theory based upon the principle of reciprocity, on the notion of operant conditioning or on the utilitarian concept of mutually rewarding exchanges do not seem to cover this theoretical ground. There is, as Parsons at least saw, a problem of order which cannot be ignored. More than this we have found it necessary to go beyond Parsons to consider what occurs when order breaks down.

3

CONFLICT AND SOCIAL SYSTEMS

The concepts of system and action

In what has gone before our theorising has been cast in terms of a model of dyadic interpersonal interaction. That is to say that the 'atoms' of our theory have been hypothetical individual actors, the mutual orientation of whose action is thought of as bringing social relations into being. Such an approach to conflict has been held by some to be inadequate in that it is argued that it deals only with social conflict and not systems conflict[1] or that it deals with conflict at the expense of the related concept of contradiction.[2] Therefore, we must now consider the relationship of the concept of conflict to that of social systems.

The concept of system is a concept which has widespread usage in all science, not merely in the social sciences and in sociology.[3] It was also taken over in its natural science usage by Talcott Parsons from the physiologist Henderson[4] and greatly affected Parsons' later work.[5] Parsons, it is true, insists in his discussion of Pareto[6] that the concept of system is used by analogy and is free of the '"reductive" tendencies so prominent in the older positivism', but it does seem that in his subsequent writings the functional sub-systems which make up the social system are looked at in a natural science framework and involve little reference to the kind of meaningful action which would be central to any methodological individualist approach. Similarly, there is no such reference to meaningful action in the use of the concept of system to refer to a structured totality within the modern traditions of structuralism. Deriving as it does from linguistics, this tradition is basically concerned with relationships of meaning divorced from action, and even Gidden's attempt to relate such an approach to action through the concept of structuration does not involve meaningful action as we understand it.

A methodological individualist approach to socio-cultural systems

An analysis of socio-cultural systems which does distinguish itself from the general scientific usage of the term 'system' and which looks at institutions as meaningful is the older and in many ways less sophisticated analysis of Malinowski. We shall now look at his analysis and show how it might be modified to allow for conflict and go on to show how, in the later formulations of Radcliffe-Brown and Robert Merton, some of Malinowski's insights were lost.[7]

At the outset it will be necessary to note that there has been considerable divergence in the usage of the terms 'institution', 'association', 'group' and 'community'. A group may be thought of, following Max Weber,[8] as a complex of social relations of a more or less systematic kind with or without the additional features of representation and leadership. It assumes stability of interaction of some kind between a plurality of persons between whom and the outside world there is some degree of closure. The distinction between 'association' and 'community' is derived from Tönnies[9] and is closely followed in the basic text of MacIver and Page.[10] According to MacIver and Page, 'a community is an area of social living marked by some degree of social coherence'. Its bases are 'locality and community sentiment'. Also implicit in their definition is the notion that a community exists for a multitude of diffuse ends. In contrast, an 'association' is a 'group organised for the pursuit of an interest or a group of interests in common'.

By contrast, for MacIver and Page, institutions may be looked upon from an impersonal point of view. They are 'established forms or conditions of procedure characteristic of group activity'. They are a part of the cultural heritage rather than of the interactive systems which we refer to by the terms 'society', 'group', 'association' and 'community'. Since they often have a normative force it is quite common to equate the terms 'norms' and 'institutions', the term 'institutions' being especially reserved for norms which govern behaviour in some especially important area of co-operative activity whether within an association or a community.

In Parsons' *The Social System*, the social system is one of three interacting systems, the cultural, the social and the personality system. None actually operates in isolation from the others and the social is bound in by the cultural. The cultural can be studied for its own sake and would appear to be the special province of cultural anthropology. So far as the sociologist is concerned, however, culture and the normative order constitute an input into the social systems and the norms form part of the binding-in of social relations which Parsons calls 'institutionalisation'.

The identification of 'institutions' with the normative order is taken for granted by Lockwood in his critique of Parsons.[11] As against Parsons, he argues that the normative structuring of social interaction is only one aspect of the social and that this needs to be supplemented by a study of the underlying infrastructure of factual constraints and interests.

Malinowski, in arguing that institutions are the legitimate isolate of cultural analysis, extends the usage of the term so as to locate them within a framework of organised purposive activities interpreted as associations and also to refer to the material base of this activity. Whether or not this usage is a correct one from the point of view of the general sociological literature, it is useful in that it combines within a single analysis the cultural or normative, the social and the material. It is this fact that enables us to use it in the analysis of various types of conflict within institutions and between institutions.

One preliminary difficulty about Malinowski's analysis may be set aside. This concerns its relation in terms of institutions to an analysis in terms of groups. As Parsons has pointed out [12] and, as is clear from contradictions within Malinowski's own posthumously published and incomplete text,[13] institutions are organised forms of activity which may be performed by different groups or which may draw their personnel from the same group. Thus the breakdown of the society in terms of groups based upon kinship, age, authority, territory and so on does not coincide with the placement of personnel for role performance within institutions. In simple societies especially, the kinship system carries with it sets of rights and duties which provide the role structure of a range of institutions.

The main significance of Malinowski's theory, of course, lies in his distinction between the declared purpose or charter of a patterned form of institutional activity and its 'function' or the unrecognised purpose which it serves for an individual or for the system, and it is this distinction which Merton repeats when he speaks of manifest and latent functions.[14] The point which we should notice here, however, is simply that both charter and function are specifically teleological terms. Malinowski does not seek, as some of his successors do, to conceal the difference between functional and causal explanations (or, more exactly, explanations in terms of effect behind the unexplicated term 'need'). Moreover, the teleological element in this explanation refers not simply to the needs of some supra-individual system but to the needs of a 'methodological' or theoretical individual from whose standpoint the systematic interconnections of the system are being analysed.

Malinowski's system is not primarily normative. Its end point of reference is a biological one or a material one. That is to say that directly or indirectly the functions of all institutions are to satisfy the biological or survival needs of individuals. Thus, on one level at least, it appears to take account of the infrastructure to which Lockwood refers. As we shall see it also takes account of this infrastructure on other levels.

The elements of Malinowski's tentative system are well enough known. They include a diagram indicating what are, in one sense, the theoretical elements involved in organised institutional activity and, in another, an indication to the fieldworker, with whose empirical orientation Malinowski was always concerned, of a set of headings under which data and explanations should be recorded. Secondly, they indicate the way in which secondary institutions are related to primary ones and, in a more shadowy way in an incomplete section, the role of possible tertiary institutions.

A basic institution is to be thought of as having the following elements: charter, personnel, norms, material apparatus, activities and functions. Central to these is the notion of 'activities'. Activities are, in the first place, what the fieldworker discovers his subjects to be doing. But Malinowski is not a behaviourist, pure and simple. Observed behaviour is interpreted in terms of an action schema in which there is a conscious goal (recorded in the 'charter') in which material means are used (the material apparatus), in which the conduct of a hypothetical actor takes account of the behaviour of others (the personnel) and the action sequence is thought to be governed by norms. In short the whole action schema fulfils the requirements laid down by Parsons as appropriate for a theory of action.[15] The basic institution concept taken by itself however, does not imply that the actor around whose action this concept is built necessarily has his ends and means modified in such a way that his action coincides with that of actors acting out other institutional activities. The possibility of conflict is thus far kept open.

The emphasis upon the material apparatus draws attention to an important element which is underplayed in Parsons' reference to means and conditions. In seeking to oppose positivist theories which reduce normative factors to means and conditions, Parsons overemphasises the normative. It is clear that in Malinowski's schema, on the other hand, the material apparatus and the normative structure have equal importance. This would appear to meet Lockwood's strictures on the Parsonian system. It also implicitly suggests a source of conflict within institutions.

In inserting the term 'personnel' along with norms, Malinowski draws attention, as Parsons does, to the interrelation between a purely social or interactive element and a cultural one. Moreover, the neutral term 'personnel' leaves open the question of whether what is involved here is an organised group, a market mechanism or some other sort of multi-person structure of a more or less co-operative, more or less conflictual kind.

The norms to which Malinowski refers are of two kinds. On the one hand there is the patterning of behaviour involved in the pursuit of the activity in terms of technical, moral and aesthetic criteria. On the other there is the normative structure which has to be taken account of by the personnel in ordering their conduct to one another.

We need not spend much time on the 'charter'. Its presence in Malinowski's schema is intended mainly to draw attention to the fact that it is not from a scientific point of view a very important element. The very term used suggests a largely irrelevant piece of parchment. Its main use may simply be to legitimate the relevant action and it belongs, in a sense, to the tertiary level of institutions which we shall discuss below.

'Function', unlike the other elements in Malinowski's schema, involves not merely description but explanation. As a fieldworker Malinowski did not devote any attention to the problems involved in proving statements about function. What he did was merely to advise other fieldworkers that they should be prepared to offer such explanations *ad hoc* and to consider at the moment of observation the possibility that activities could be serving a purpose other than that enshrined in the charter.

In his inevitably oversimplified schema Malinowski suggested that there were seven basic sets of needs, viz. metabolism, reproduction, bodily comforts, safety, movement, growth and health, which had to be met if a population was to survive, and seven cultural responses involving institutions, called respectively commissariat, kinship, shelter, protection, activities training and hygiene. What is important here, however, is not whether Malinowski's list is exhaustive or correct but that he suggests that there are purposes concerned with biological survival which determine the kinds of organised institutional response that there must be. Difficulties, however, might arise which are relevant to our main theme, if the fulfilment of one need prevents the fulfilment of another or if the satisfaction of the needs of some individuals conflict with the satisfaction of the needs of others.

So far all that has been said is that any society must organise routinised ways of providing for basic needs and that if one understands that this is a survival imperative for the members of a society, much of the recurrently observed activity will make sense in relation to this imperative. In the oversimplified model it is as though the society was thought of as having a series of committees to deal purposively with these problems.

The secondary institutions and social reproduction

Social organisation, however, implies social reproduction and the primary institutions have to be sustained by secondary ones. In the case of the secondary institutions, however, the function, instead of being to provide for the biological needs of individuals, is to provide for the renewal of the elements of the basic ones. Otherwise they have the same elements of charter, personnel, norms, material apparatus and activities. It should also be noted, however, that they must service one another.

There is a rough correspondence between the kinds of secondary institutions and the elements involved in the basic ones. A political institution provides for the reproduction of the role system labelled personnel; a legal institution sustains the normative system; what Malinowski calls the 'economic system' maintains and renews the material apparatus; and the educational institution provides for the instruction of newcomers in the appropriate activities.

Separately from these secondary institutions, and having a different relationship to basic and secondary institutions is the tertiary institution. Its function, it may be said, is to maintain the charter system. Being furthest removed from the satisfaction of biological needs it may seem the least important, but since individuals consciously pursue 'charter' aims rather than functional ones it is vitally important for the system that these be sustained. Thus there is some uncertainty in Malinowski's system as to whether these are purely derivative institutions or whether they are the primary ones on which the continuance of the whole system depends.

The revision of Malinowski by conflict theory

Malinowski was a functionalist. Indeed many would argue that he was the founding father of functionalism. His aim, therefore, was to show how all institutions were interconnected in a system (albeit an open system which responded to external biological imperatives). What we now have to do, as we did in dealing with Parsons' concept of the dyad, is to show how his model might be developed to account for conflict.

There are a number of points at which conflict might occur within the system. These include conflicts between different biological goals and the biological goals of different individuals and groups, conflicts and contradictions between the institutional elements, especially between the material apparatus on the one hand and the norms on the other, conflicts within the personnel and conflicts between the actual output of various institutions and the functional needs which they are supposed to serve. We shall deal with each of these in turn.

In the first place we have to notice the fact of scarcity. Malinowski offers us a model in which there is no conflict between the basic institutions. Each satisfies a need and satisfies it fully for the whole population involved. In fact, however, particularly when the same 'personnel' are involved in several institutions there is a problem of 'economising' (i.e. choosing between needs to be satisfied in varying degrees) and a problem of distribution (i.e. deciding whose needs will be satisfied). Malinowski tells us what is necessary for minimal survival, i.e. the sufficient satisfaction of the needs of a sufficient proportion of the population to keep the whole system manned. This, however, may involve a death-rate and resistance on the part of those who are about to die. It will also be the case that improved technology permits a higher level of need satisfaction and that a further problem of distributing the surplus will arise.

A change in the material apparatus through technological innovation which is external to Malinowski's conservative social system may well imply a new arrangement of the roles which constitute the personnel system and also render inappropriate the norms which governed activities prior to the innovation. If, at this point, the old personnel and norms are maintained, the potentialities of the new technology may not be realised. In such circumstances those who realise that the potential of the technology for satisfying their needs at a higher level might well have an interest in and seek to institute a new role system and a new normative order.

Most interesting of all perhaps is the question of the structure of the 'personnel'. Malinowski here assumes stable groups or a kinship system which provides a fixed and stable role system overall. The personnel may, however, be so arranged that they compete with or come into conflict with one another. Such competition and conflict may be institutionalised so that competition and conflict are the normal means whereby needs are satisfied and the problems of economising and distribution solved. Or the system may be sufficiently unstable for processes such as those we have discussed in the last two chapters to be initiated and pursued until a new equilibrium is reached.

Given that there is conflict amongst the personnel, what may follow at the secondary level will not so much be social reproduction of the system but social reproduction of the conflict. Thus there will be not one political, one legal, one technological and one educational system but two in each case, in conflict with one another.

The sort of situation which we have in mind is well illustrated when we try to apply Durkheim's theory of religion to modern societies. Durkheim sees religion as sustaining a stable social structure by making its institutions sacred. But, as Richard Niebuhr has shown,[16] many Christian sects and denominations may have the form and content of religions of the disinherited as well as of the establishment. Similarly deprived groups may well seek to educate their own members for the struggle against their oppressors.

Societies and classes as socio-cultural systems

When such a division runs throughout the secondary institutions of a society we may speak of a counter-culture. In such a case the 'personnel' of the various secondary and basic institutions are likely to be in touch with another and, instead of constituting a single social framework of interrelated roles called 'society', constitute two alternative and opposed networks called classes. This may indeed be one of the most significant meanings which can be attached in sociology to the term 'class'. In Marxian terms we might say that when personnel in conflict across the board in primary and secondary institutions relate to each other in this way we have 'classes-in-themselves'.

Conflict between institutions

Separately from this type of conflict, however, we have to consider the case in which not merely the separate elements within an institution contradict or are in conflict with one another but in which the different institutions have an output or achieve effects which are 'dysfunctional' for other institutions. Such conflicts and contradictions inevitably arise because, as Engels saw, even institutions which were not part of the economic base, take on a life of their own and are not immediately responsive to changes in the institutions which they came into being to serve. Moreover, as Weber saw, these institutions might produce personnel who constituted a status group with its own way of life which achieved a certain ascendancy in the society as a whole as in the case of the literati of China or the Brahmins of India.[17] Any historically applicable sociological theory has to take account of these phenomena and cannot rest content with a simplistic functionalism.

The role of the 'economic' and the 'infrastructure'

Lockwood seeks to distinguish his account of system-integration and system-contradiction from that which emphasises dysfunction by arguing that there is the possibility of latent contradiction between the material infrastructure and the 'institutional' level in any institution.[18] According to the account presented here both types of contradiction or conflict are important. The terms 'material infrastructure' and 'institutions' perhaps serve to conceal the difference.

It may be appropriate at this point to note again that the distinction between 'contradiction' and 'conflict' is not of great importance from a methodological individualist point of view. The units which come into 'contradiction' here are thought of as organised forms of purposive activity. As such they lead naturally to the notion of conflicts over ends and means. The emphasis on the term 'contradiction' is one which derives via Marxism from the philosophy of Hegel and hence confuses the analysis of sequences and clashes of patterns of action with logical contradiction. This has some meaning in Hegelian thought, but only serves to cloud and confuse sociological analysis.

One last point should be made about Malinowski's theory which also relates to Marxism. This is his use of the term 'economic'. Writing, as he was, about simple societies based on kinship, he saw the economic as being concerned with the material apparatus, and production and the reproduction of the material apparatus. In modern societies, however, the term is ambiguously used. It refers to production it is true, but especially to production for the market and it is primarily the network of social interactions which occurs in the market-place which are termed 'economic'. The 'economy' is thought of as the system of exchange relationships which goes on in the market, and this clearly is the main way in which modern capitalist societies satisfy their needs. But it is also possible to speak of a society's 'technology' which has its own separate imperatives. A full development and application of Malinowski's theory would have to allow then for both the economy (a particular structure of 'personnel') and for technology. In fact we might have to treat the economy as an intermediate institution, intermediate between the basic and the secondary ones and one which perhaps exercises an influence greater than any other throughout the system.

The functionalist tradition after Malinowski: Radcliffe-Brown and Merton

We may now use this analysis of the elements in Malinowski's theory as a basis for understanding some of the problems inherent in other theories. First we shall say something about the continuation of the functionalist tradition in the work of Radcliffe-Brown and Merton and then go on to consider the structural–functionalism of Parsons and the functionalist aspects of Marxism.

Radcliffe-Brown[19] rejects Malinowski's apparent biological determinism and argues that social anthropology should be concerned solely with *social* functions. He thus offers us a closed as opposed to an open systems theory. The twin concepts in his theory are those of structure and function. An activity is explained by showing that the effect of its performance is to maintain the structure. The term 'function' is justified in that failure does not merely mean different effects but that the structure collapses or dies. 'Structure' refers above all in primitive societies to the network of social relations implied by the kinship system. Some similar structure has to be located as the starting-point in advanced societies. Such a structure appears to be the network of market relations.

Because this is an open rather than a closed systems theory it cannot really allow for conflict at all. The final reference point is the structure, and none of the points of strain that result from Malinowski's formulation of his theory of the socio-cultural system as a system of organised purposive activity come to the surface.

The only equivalent in Radcliffe-Brown's formulation to latent conflict in Malinowski's is the notion of sickness and death which derives from the analogy between societies and organisms. The one imperative is that the structure should be maintained and 'live' 'healthily'. But precisely here the analogy breaks down. If what happens in the social sphere were to happen amongst organisms, as Radcliffe-Brown admits, a pig, instead of growing ill or dying, might be transmuted into a hippopotamus. Surely some account must be given of this kind of transition, and what account can be given but to say that in societies we have conflict rather than illness.

Merton is generally regarded, and rightly, as the sociologist who released functionalism from the charge of conservative teleology by introducing the notion of dysfunction. This is one of the directions in which Malinowski's and Radcliffe-Brown's theory has to be modified in order to allow for conflict and change. It is, however, only one amongst several, and Merton himself recognised others when he argued that it was necessary to say exactly to what part of a social structure an activity was functional or dysfunctional[20]. Here he also appears to have in mind conflicts of ends because he uses the instance of industrial practices which are functional to management but dysfunctional to the workers.

Despite this it would seem that Merton does not break out of the kind of closed-systems theory advocated by Radcliffe-Brown. It remains a part of his paradigm for functional analysis to demonstrate the 'needs' of the system even though he admits that 'this remains one of the cloudiest and empirically most debatable concepts in functional theory.[21]

Parson's systems theory

Parsons' functionalism operates on different levels in his earlier and later work. In *The Social System* the emphasis is still on the structure of social interaction and on the way in which different patterns of action orientation and social relations are contained within a stable social system. Here Parsons still works within the action frame of reference. In his later work, however, it is not structures of action and relationships which constitute the units of the system but four functional sub-systems.

Parsons would no doubt claim that his is an open type of systems theory in that each of the sub-systems deals on behalf of the social systems as a whole with the external environment. The adaptive system is concerned with the mobilisation of facilities; the goal-attainment system is concerned with goals which may be outside the system; the integrative system relates the social and cultural systems; and the pattern-maintenance and tension-management system relates the social and personality systems. But there is not the same kind of openness as in Malinowski's system. The social system is a boundary-maintaining one and the sub-systems are seen primarily as producing services, resources and facilities for one another. It is not thought of as a quasi-organic system like Radcliffe-Brown's, yet like his theory it sees the purpose of the sub-systems as primarily concerned with keeping each other and the whole social system going.

Characteristic of this approach is the treatment of the products of the sub-systems as resources for the system as a whole. The adaptive system produces the generalised facility called income; the goal-attainment system produces the other most important generalised resource, power; the integrative system produces 'solidarity'; and the pattern-maintenance and tension-management system value-orientation. In our view money and power are sought after and possessed by individuals and groups, solidarity arises in relation to the pursuit of goals and the value-orientations are understood as a means of maintaining motivation (as in the case of Malinowski's tertiary institution).

System contradiction and class conflict in Marx

Marxist theory appears, as in most ways, the very antithesis of Parsonian. It begins with human labour and sees most of what

Parsons regards as resources of the system merely as alienated labour. Its aim is the demystification of theories like Parsons'. It emphasises system-contradiction rather than system-maintenance and it posits class conflict both as endemic in capitalist society and as the means of transition to a new social order. None the less Marx wrote, even in his later works, in a vocabulary strongly influenced by Hegelianism and it is necessary to restate it and to seek to clarify it in terms of a more general sociological vocabulary.

In his early work Marx addressed himself to the philosophic problem of alienation and, in the 1860s, to the specific problems of political economy. As early as 1845, however, he wrote in the *Theses on Feuerbach* that 'the human essence is the ensemble of social relations' and thereby appeared to be concerned above all with the development of sociological theory. His later work is also to be understood not simply as an exercise in political economy, but as an attempt to get behind the mystification of the economists to the reality of social relations.

The mature statement of the sociological position underlying *Das Kapital* is to be found in Marx's *Preface to A Contribution to the Critique of Political Economy* of 1859. There he writes as follows:

In the social productions of their life, men enter into definite relations that are indispensable and independent of their will, relations of production which correspond to a definite stage of the development of productive forces. The sum total of these relations of production constitutes the economic structure of society, the real foundation, on which arises a legal and political superstructure and to which correspond definite forms of social consciousness. The mode of production of material life conditions the social, political and intellectual life process in general. It is not the consciousness of men that determines their being, but on the contrary their social being that determines their consciousness. At a certain stage of their development the productive forces of society come in conflict with the existing social relations of production, or – what is but a legal expression of the same thing – with the property relations within which they have been at work hitherto. From forms of development of the productive forces these relations turn into their fetters. Then begins an epoch of social revolution. With the change of the economic foundation the entire immense superstructure is more or less rapidly transformed. In considering such transformations distinction should always be made between the material transformation of the economic conditions of production which can be determined with the precision of natural science and the legal, political, religious, aesthetic or philosophic – in short ideological forms in which men become conscious of this conflict and fight it out. . . . No social order ever perishes before all the productive forces for which there is room in it have developed; and new higher relations of production never appear before the material conditions of existence have matured in the womb of the old society itself.[22]

These words are too often quoted with scriptural reverence. In fact, precisely because they are important for sociological theory, it is necessary to clarify them, distinguishing the sociological core from what amounts to philosophical asides or mere rhetoric.

One starts here, not as with Malinowski with the concept of biological needs, but with the more obscure and ambiguous notion of men's social production of their life. This *might* be interpreted as meaning 'satisfying their basic needs', but the whole of Marx's thought is directed against such a conception. Man is regarded as different from the animals in that he expresses his nature in production. It is this labouring productive man whom Marx opposes to Hegel's Spirit as the main agent of history.

Two points may be made in favour of placing 'production' at the centre of any sociological analysis. Firstly, it is true that it is part of the human condition that unlike the animals man does have to work to satisfy most of his basic biological needs. Secondly, it is more and more the case that, as men's level of aspiration in the satisfaction of their needs rises organised production as distinct from more spasmodic activity comes to be central in his life. Marx was also right in recognising that while labour was a burden which men had to bear it also gave him the possibility of increasing his standard of life, a point which is missing in Malinowski's theory. Putting production at the centre makes possible the understanding of evolution and change.

Simple evolutionary change, however, is ruled out for Marx by the second part of the first sentence which we have quoted, for in the process of production men enter social relations which are 'independent of their will'. Thus men lose their freedom. They are confronted with an alien social force, which means in effect that conflict is inherent in this most basic human activity.

But what are these social relations and is Marx correct in saying that they are independent of the producer's will?

Clearly, it is possible to conceive of social relations or co-operative activity as freely chosen and indeed as giving additional satisfactions to those which derive from 'production'. Two factors, however, stand in the way. One is that, although in the first instance these social relations may be freely chosen they may come to rest upon the distribution of property and power. The second is that what they are or can be will depend upon and correspond to 'a particular stage in the development of the forces of production'. The first of these factors suggests social alienation, the second alienation through technology.

Clearly, Marx does not believe that social alienation is man's ultimate destiny. The social relations which appear to constrain him from outside are made by men and can be changed by men. But this will require fighting against the sanctions which attach to the social relations of production through revolution.

The possibility of such revolution, however, is qualified by the final phrase. These relations correspond to a certain stage in the development of the productive forces and, later in the quoted passage, Marx says explicitly: 'No social order ever perishes before all the productive forces for which there is room in it have developed.' Thus the question must be asked whether Marx was in fact a technological determinist.

The charge of technological determinism is one which Marxists hotly deny and it is suggested that the terms 'forces of production' refer to more than mere technology. One can appreciate the difficulty which they face, for they wish to do justice to the materialist basis of Marxism, yet at the same time to insist upon the importance of activity and social relations in Marx's whole philosophical orientation. Marx did distinguish his own type of materialism from that of Feuerbach by insisting that the 'matter' which was important for him was 'sensuous human activity'.[23] None the less, at this point a distinction has to be made between a technology which implies a division of labour on the one hand and the social framework or the 'social relations of production' which stand opposed to it.

If Marxists are anxious that the concept of 'forces of production' should not be construed as a purely material element, they are equally anxious that the social relations of production should not be construed as a purely social one. These social relations have to be opposed not merely to the forces of production but to ideological forms which constitute the superstructure of which they are the real foundation or basis. We thus have a double relationship which is expressed in Fig. 2.

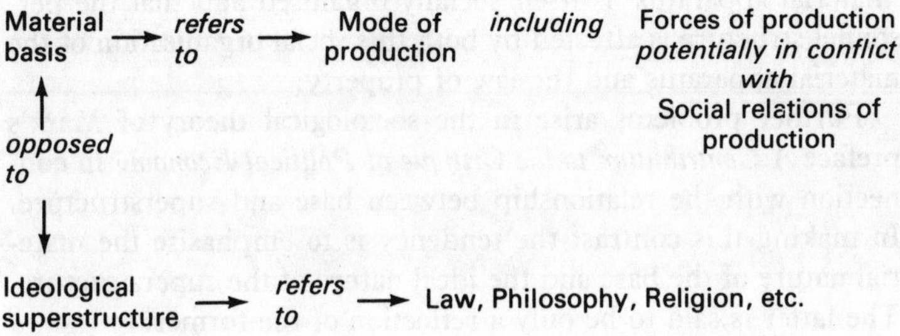

Material basis → *refers to* → Mode of production *including* Forces of production *potentially in conflict with* Social relations of production

↑ *opposed to* ↓

Ideological superstructure → *refers to* → Law, Philosophy, Religion, etc.

Fig. 2

In fact, however, it is possible to distinguish between the social relations of production and the ideological superstructure in a different way without declaring the social relations of production to be 'material'. Social relations never can be purely 'material'. They consist of expectations and responses to those expectations, as we have seen in Chapter 1. These social relations, however, are seen as different from others in that they are concerned with production and rest upon the inequalities of the property system backed by political power. This is an important difference which is probably only confused by calling the differentiating feature 'material'. For Marx what was important was the emphasis upon production and upon property. Because he was engaged in the Idealist/Materialist debate in philosophy he was inclined to hold production as material and property, or at least the law of property, somewhat more ambiguously as ideal or ideological.

Marxist theory and the language of sociology

The problems here may be clarified by relating Marx's account to Malinowski's schema. What we are talking about is production, an institution whose 'function' is generalised need satisfaction. Such an institution uses a material apparatus and has a personnel. Relations between the personnel are subject to norms, but it is characteristic of these norms that they rest upon and justify a particular property system. What Marxism does as compared with Malinowski's simple theory is to suggest that the 'material apparatus' is itself socially organised and that the personnel structure is affected by both this social organisation of the material apparatus and the law of property.

Further problems arise in the sociological theory of Marx's preface *A Contribution to the Critique of Political Economy* in connection with the relationship between base and superstructure. In making this contrast the tendency is to emphasise the material nature of the base and the ideal nature of the superstructure. The latter is said to be only a reflection of the former.

What is lacking here is an adequate sociological language for talking about social relations and social institutions. We would wish to suggest that both the base and the superstructure have an institutional form. In the base, or the institution of production, there is a unique function, namely that of providing generalised need satisfaction, and there is obviously a much closer dependence upon the material apparatus, but there is also a system of social relations, albeit one heavily influenced by power and property distribution. In the superstructure there are a number of institutions which serve to support and reproduce the elements of the base, but they do not consist simply of disembodied ideas. They consist of organised activities carried on by a personnel within a definite structure of social relations and even, though to a lesser extent than in the institution of production, dependent upon their own material apparatus. Marx, engaged in a lifelong polemic against Hegelian philosophy, naturally tended to characterise the secondary range of institutions in the terms in which Hegel characterised them, that is as representing developing forms of Idea or Spirit. For our generation, amongst which Hegelianism has little significance, it becomes important to characterise them differently, all the more so because the problem of their relative importance remains. That is to say we do not prove their relative unimportance by discussing them as mere ideas. We have to argue that, even though they have institutional form they have less determining influence on the social system as a whole than the institution of production.

The question of economic determinism restated

There are probably, in fact, very few sociologists today, whether Marxist or non-Marxist, who would argue that a distinction cannot be drawn between basic institutions which have a relatively determining role in the structure of the social system and other institutions which are relatively dependent. On the other hand many contemporary Marxists[24] are anxious to insist that they do not believe that there is a simple immediate relation of determination and dependence. A widely accepted formulation is that 'practices' other than production do take on a life of their own and that it is even possible that in a particular 'social formation', although the whole system is ultimately dependent upon production, one of the other practices may be 'in dominance' so long as the social formation lasts. This gives considerable flexibility to Marxist sociological thinking and goes as far as is necessary in responding to the charge of economic determinism.

Again it is important to emphasise the distinction between conflict and contradiction between the elements of the basic institutions of production and wider system or interinstitutional conflict and contradiction. Marxism is unable to articulate this difference clearly because it lacks any term equivalent to that of 'institution' as it is used by Malinowski. Restatement of the theory in terms of a richer sociological vocabularly actually helps to emphasise its importance and raise more subtle problems for analysis.

The emphasis in the passage from Marx's preface is always on system-conflict rather than intergroup or class conflict. Marx would, in his political writings of the early 1850s, have placed more emphasis upon the latter. Strangely, however, after he became preoccupied with the problems of economic theory, he ceased to talk much about class formation. In our terms, however, there is a way in which class conflict can be built into Marx's system. If, as we have said, conflict exists between the parties who constitute the personnel of the productive system and that conflict produces equivalent conflict in the secondary or superstructural institutions then the personnel of all these institutions taken together constitute not merely a class, but in Marxist terms a 'class-for-itself' or a self-conscious class, and such class formation is then available when contradiction between the forces and social relations of production makes the maintenance of the old social relations impossible.

It may be asked, of course, whether conflict theory should not allow a place for conflict which goes on in any institution at all, whether of the base or superstructure. Of course it should. Modern Marxism, moreover, is accommodating on this point. According to Althusser 'contradictions' (we should say 'conflicts') might appear at any point in the system, and social breakdown and revolutionary change will occur not simply because there is contradiction in the base (that may occur without inducing change) but when the weight of contradictions overall is such (when the contradictions are so 'overdetermined') that the system as a whole must change.[25] It would seem, therefore, that the study of conflicts within other institutions and practices are not only a permissible extra but an essential part of modern Marxism.

So far we have assumed that the system of production and the social relations to which it gives rise are the ultimate basis on which all other institutions arise. But there are certain parts of Marx's writings, most notably in *Das Kapital*, which suggest that a kind of Marxism needs to be written which goes beyond this. The analysis of the productive system was, after all, the accomplishment of the bourgeois economists, and Marx wrote *Das Kapital* as a critique of political economy. His aim was to demystify the understanding of the economy which the bourgeois economists thought they had achieved. He did this by claiming to show that the whole system which economics described depended upon the alienation of labour from the worker and the extraction of surplus value. Thus there are Marxists who claim that it is misleading of some French Marxists to plead for the relative autonomy of the political. Marx, it is said, had never in fact been an economic determinist at all, and what Marxism has to do is to show how both the economy and the polity rest upon some more fundamental sub-stratum of social relations. The revisionism of French Marxists therefore seems to give to the polity an independence which Marx had not even claimed for the economy.[26]

The trouble with this approach is that it probably demystifies too much. When the organised system of social relations in all institutions has been demystified away, what remains are the purest forms of interaction of all unstructured by any institutional or normative order. Whether such a world constitutes a Hobbesian war of all against all or not would depend upon one's view of human nature. On the other hand, it might be argued that what was important at this level was power and violence which would come to be expressed in a property system.

Such positions are understandable and there is no way in which we can determine the final truth in one way or another. Surely it would be a sensible version of Marxism which argued that the institutions of production were basic to the social system, but that the social framework within which production was carried on was structured in terms of a system of power and property. That is to say, the economy includes a political element. Marx's own political practice suggests very strongly that this was his view. He knew that the economy was important, but he wanted to repoliticise it rather than accept it as given according to the laws of nature.

Marxism's unique contribution to conflict theory

All in all we can see that Marxist theory has important contributions to make to the theory of social conflict. It is unique in placing at the centre of its system of institutional analysis the institution of production, but sees that institution as dependent both upon technological and political factors. It raises for us the notion of new social relations latent in a technology and envisages the development of conflict and contradiction between these latent social relations and those which currently exist. It suggests a complex relationship between institutions which are basic and those which are superstructural. Finally, while giving pre-eminence in its later forms to system-conflict, it suggests a relationship between such conflict and the conflict between persons and classes.

Since none of the functionalist theories which we have discussed, including Malinowski's, has much to say about these various aspects of conflict, we would certainly see Marxism as a major source for sociological conflict theory. In order that it should be fully developed, however, Marxism needs to be liberated from its essentially Hegelian problematic and terminology and enriched by a modern sociological vocabulary which refers to action, social relations and social institutions.

Conflict in functionalist theory

The kind of theory of conflict which we have been suggesting is, by its very nature, a theory of social disruption and social change. Finally, something should therefore be said about the rather unexpected theory that conflict contributes to the stability of social systems.[27]

This type of theory arose in rather specific historical circumstances in the mid-1950s. Sociological theory of that time, under the influence particularly of Parsons, placed so much emphasis upon order that it appeared to suggest that all conflict or even dissent was dangerous, if not treasonable. In the political arena in America the phenomenon of McCarthyism reinforced the same point in practical terms. Liberal-minded sociologists therefore found themselves defending the essence of liberal democracy which, as they envisaged it, allowed for dissent and for political and industrial conflict and bargaining. Three types of argument were used. Conflict was said to reinforce norms and bring them to life; it was not disruptive because conflicts cross-cut one another and did not threaten the political order; and conflict provided a safety valve. Separately from this it was argued, starting from Simmel's sociology, that associative and dissociative elements existed in all social relationships.

The most relevant of these arguments is that which relates conflict to the normative structure. This is easily understandable in terms of what we have said in our first chapter. Clearly, when norms no longer correspond to the balance of power they are unworkable and there is a danger if attempts are made to enforce them that they will eventually provoke conflict of a disruptive kind. If, however, conflict occurs early and legitimately, the norms may be modified and acquire new strength because they rest upon the new *de facto* balance of power. It obviously is the case, for example, that a freely negotiated wages system will have greater legitimacy than one which is imposed in an authoritarian way. In making this valid point, however, some sociologists have tacitly ignored the possibility that the modification of the norms proposed might involve radical transformation of the system as a whole. To deny this might have been good tactics in the face of McCarthyism, but it provided the basis of only a limited sociology of conflict.

The second argument is that which rests upon the notion of cross-cutting conflicts. If one's enemy on one front is one's ally on another, it is argued, each particular conflict will necessarily be limited because despite that conflict bonds have to be preserved with one's present enemy. This is true enough. But it is not universally the case that conflicts do cancel each other out in this way in modern industrial society. They may, if they are to be fully pursued, coalesce, producing class politics. In these circumstances the notion of cross-cutting conflicts may actually be a strategy of the powerful to divide and rule the relatively powerless. Again a systematic sociology of conflict has to take into account these other possibilities.[28]

The notion of conflict as a safety-valve is less important. In fact it takes conflict less than seriously or assigns it purely to the psychological level. Implicit in this notion is the idea that conflict is due to strain and personality disturbance and that the goals of the resisting party are unreal.[29] One therefore allows the dissident to let off steam and by so doing ensures his adaptation to the *status quo*. A much more radical version of this type of argument would be that 'letting off steam' must be allowed either to allow for adaptation and learning or to ensure that conflict was pursued on a rational non-affective basis.

The more general reflection that there are associative and dissociative aspects in all social relations is simply true. This by no means requires, however, that we should not analyse them separately. Unintentionally no doubt, Gluckman,[30] for instance, puts this notion to ideological use when he detects associative tendencies in oppressive relations such as those embodied in the South

African colour bar. One might just as well draw the opposite conclusion and see dissociative and conflictual tendencies in situations of apparent consensus. What we have to do as sociologists is to project models both of the maintenance of order and of the pursuit of conflict, and the latter must by no means stop short at any conflict leading to disruption and change.

In short, the theory of the 'functions of social conflict' is a part, but only a small part, of the total theory of conflict. What is more, we have shown in this chapter that systems theory which deals only with order and stability is only a part of systems theory. Conflict, too, can be systematic, and part of the task of the sociologist is to show how systems involve the possibility of conflict between these parts and conflict between individuals and groups which may modify or fundamentally change the system.

4

COLLECTIVITIES IN CONFLICT

In earlier chapters we have written generally about the theory of social conflict as it applies to conflicts between individual actors and between collectivities. We must now turn, however, to the question of the capacity of different kinds of collectivities to enter into conflict as collective actors.

Nation states as actors in conflict

Theoretically the simplest case of conflict between collectivities is the case of international relations where the units are sovereign nation states. It is also the case above all in which conflict must take precedence over consensus, since by definition the sovereign state keeps peace within its own borders, but recognises that beyond them it has no monopoly of the means of physical coercion so that order, if there be any, must rest upon the balance of power.

The state as a compulsory association

International order is quite unlike the market situation which we described in Chapter 2. If the representatives of State A do not find acceptable what the representatives of State B have to offer, they cannot simply look for alternative 'suppliers', i.e. other citizens of State B who would make a better offer. Anyone claiming to make such an offer would be seen as guilty of subversion, if not treason. This is to say that the nation state is a compulsory association and one which empowers its representatives to speak on behalf of the whole membership. It is important to understand this, not merely in order to understand the nation state itself, but in order to understand the true nature of conflict between non-compulsory and imperfect associations and communities.

One should note, however, that even in the case of nation states, the assumption of the universal loyalty of their citizens cannot always be made. Although states profess not to interfere in each other's internal affairs there is a margin within which they do. Such interference is thought to be not only illegal in the society in which it occurs but improper according to the code of conduct which exists between nations. The political agent is usually seen as closely associated with the spy and, like him, can expect no protection from his own state if he is caught. In fact he is seen as more dangerous than the spy. The spy only finds out what policies are being pursued. The political agent tries to change them and thereby denies the sovereignty of the state in whose territory he works.

Some states, of course, have more sovereignty than others. In the struggle between the super-powers, the USA and USSR, it is usually recognised that both have satellites and clients and that interference in the affairs of its own client states by one of them will be tolerated by the other. From time to time both super-powers may propose more equal relations with their clients, but, when vital interests are threatened, intervention may be swift and sharp. There is some possibility, however, that the democratic system of the USA might make such action less likely than would be the case with the USSR which has a greater capacity for centralised decision-making, a point to which we shall have to return.

Conflict and other relations between nation states

In the case of individuals and groups within a nation normal social relations usually involve co-operation or mutually beneficial exchange, with the possibility of these breaking down into conflicts and power struggles. In the society of states the normal pattern is one of balance of power and of power conflict modified by the development of co-operative and exchange relations.

Cultural and economic exchange may take two forms. On the one hand the state itself might arrange the exchanges in the form of a bilateral agreement between states. In this case one has the equivalent in the society of states to the development of peaceful exchange relations in place of a war of all against all amongst individuals who in the first place made up the nation state. On the other hand the state may allow individuals within its area of authority to engage in exchanges with individuals in another nation state. In this case the authority of the state is inevitably undermined to some extent and a society extending across national boundaries brought into being. Such a society will exist only at the will of the sovereign states involved, however, unless a supra-national authority is set up to regulate exchanges. The European Economic Community is sometimes cited as a group of states moving towards accepting a supra-national authority, but the difficulty of such a development is illustrated by the way in which the separate states still interfere with free trade and even threaten withdrawal from the Community.

Another related area in the relations between states is that which concerns political and military alliances. On major issues in a power game which involves two super-powers there are three possibilities for a state other than the super-powers. It may align itself with Super-power A or with Super-power B or it may seek to remain neutral or non-aligned. Alliance and support may only take a weak form, such as support in a vote in the United Nations Assembly, but it may take the strong form of a military alliance in which the military involvement of one ally implies the military involvement of the other. An even stronger form of alliance involving loss of sovereignty by at least one of the states would be the setting up of a unified military command. This would usually take the form of the subordination of the military forces of one country to those of another.

The existence of cross-national exchanges of all of these types makes possible negotiation and bargaining between states well short of a power conflict or of war. The art of international relations indeed comes to life in knowing when to offer and when to withdraw an item from the exchange bargain. Thus nations may punish others who fail to comply with their wishes by withdrawing from cultural exchanges, by economic sanctions or by withdrawing military support.

International conflict of a public kind

Most such exchange and bargaining processes occur on a day-to-day basis and are known only to diplomats and others who are 'in the know'. From time to time, however, situations will arise in which there is an actual clash of wills between nation states in which it becomes necessary to take public action to compel compliance.

The lesser sanctions

One of the earliest moves of this kind is to seek to isolate the offending party from its own potential supporters. At any particular time, for example, one of the super-powers may have a certain number of satellites, other nations loosely allied and even the non-alighed countries having some limited relations with it. A public and dramatic withholding of, say, cultural exchanges by the other super-power might then be backed by an appeal to the lesser powers to alter their pattern of exchanges with the offending party. This is probably all that can be achieved by withholding cultural relations, since such relations actually benefit the offending party only through the legitimacy which they give it.

Economic sanctions

Much more serious is the withholding of trade. To the degree that a nation state has modified its own division of labour so that it actually relies upon imports of certain products, it is subject to serious pressure in this area. The two super-powers in fact limit their dependence on mutual trade of this kind and always have contingency plans for doing without any item which may be withheld in this way. Thus the withholding of Iowa grain from the USSR is likely to bring that country to its knees.

The use of economic sanctions is unlikely to be effective when used by one super-power against another. This is because they are capable, from their own resources and from those of their client states, of attaining something like self-sufficiency. Sanctions may be more effective against the lesser powers who do not have self-sufficiency within the range of their alliance. Here, however, one notices the lesser processes which go on under the super-power umbrella. In theory aligned with one of the super-powers, the medium-sized powers will also have a certain degree of independence which they will seek to cultivate and enlarge. Precisely because the super-powers single out a state for punishment by sanctions, therefore, they have the possibility of winning the support of that state by undermining sanctions. In fact the interesting point about trade sanctions is the varying degree of success with which they have been imposed. In the case of sanctions against Rhodesia or South Africa, for example, the super-powers might well find that their immediate interest is served by agreeing to sanctions in principle but not enforcing them at all severely. The very leakiness of the system might provide a card in the hand to be played at some later time. Thus it is not surprising that those who are looking for a means of compelling compliance by one of the medium-sized powers are usually cynical about the use of economic sanctions.

If economic sanctions fail to produce the required effect the next move must be to the use of force. But, even when force is contemplated we are still a long way from the ultimate in sanctions, namely the use of full-scale nuclear war by one power against another.

Military sanctions

The first moves towards the use of military force may not involve the use of the acting party's own armies at all. Many countries, particularly in the so-called Third World, are already in a state of war against internal revolution and external liberation armies. The way to bring pressure on these powers, therefore, and through them on their super-power protectors, is to increase the military resources of the revolutionaries and the guerillas. This may be done by the direct supply of arms, by financing mercenaries or by providing experts or volunteers up to the point at which eventually they actually direct the activities of the insurgents.

In order to understand what these moves mean it is necessary to understand first the concept of the balance of power amongst the super-powers. This depends upon one power possessing a stock of weapons of varying kinds deployed in appropriate places so that it is not possible for the enemy to defeat it through a pre-emptive strike.

The ultimate nuclear sanctions

The pinnacle of this system consists of nuclear weapons. According to all past thinking on military matters their potential use should serve to negate all lesser weapons, and the party which possesses the most effective of them should have the potentiality of winning any war at all. However, since the possibilities of destruction are now so great and the possibility of eliminating retaliation so slender, this logic no longer works. Hence the super-powers must resort to arms control, largely in order to work out the rules for lesser forms of warfare against a background of nuclear arms which cannot be used.

The balance of nuclear arms is, however, by no means secure as yet. There is a fear on the part of both the super-powers that the other might get itself into a position to win or at least to render itself invulnerable to nuclear attack. Moreover, the placement of weapons in strategic places would fundamentally alter the possible scenario of a nuclear war and hence of the balance of power. Such possible changes encourage the party who stands to be outclassed to take pre-emptive action.

A different problem exists in the case of the lesser powers. The possibility that the super-powers would combine to deny them a nuclear armoury is now past and a number of them, facing their own local conflicts with neighbours or insurgents, have possessed themselves of one. In some cases this must mean that they have the power to defeat, through the threat of nuclear destruction, those neighbours or insurgents who would be forced into abject surrender were it not for the possibility of obtaining nuclear protection from their allies.

Thus far the fear of nuclear destruction has resulted in nuclear weapons not being used (although this may not still be true when this book is read) and so long as this is the case, it is still possible to fight conventional wars. Such wars, however, have to be far more carefully calculated. Escalation has to occur step by step, each step being taken in the consciousness that the enemy might respond by taking a step further. This could also lead, however, not simply to controlled and limited war, but to a deliberate decision to be one step ahead of the enemy in the process of escalation.

Proxy wars

In fact the super-powers have not resorted to war between themselves for thirty-four years at the time of writing and have indeed evolved elaborate procedures for joint emergency action if the development of any conflict threatens to involve them in such a war. However, what they have been able to do is to engage in proxy wars through support for opposite sides in conflicts amongst the lesser powers.

The object of these medium-sized wars may be of two kinds. Those who prosecute the war may simply aim at getting the enemy to act or refrain from acting in a particular way or they may be seeking to install a government against his will. The first of these aims may often be achieved simply by the threat of the use of superior force. So far as the second is concerned, it is surprising how difficult it is to achieve such an aim by war. Even saturation bombing does not lead to surrender and where there is a national will to resist the struggle may be very long indeed. In the case of Vietnamese resistance, first against the French and then against the full power of the United States, resistance went on for twenty-five years and was eventually successful. However, even if the power aiming at conquest is successful, he will not automatically be able to establish an effective government. Scorched earth policies, guerilla activity and rural and urban terrorism will maintain a state of war for a very long time.

The establishment of a new regime depends above all on its capacity to achieve legitimacy in the eyes of the population just as continued resistance will depend upon establishing its illegitimacy. The route to the former will lie in a combination of firm repression of resistance with adequate rewards for compliance. Perhaps the most crucial question will be whether political figures from the old regime can be found who are prepared to declare that the new one is both a continuation of old traditions and rewarding in new ways.

What we are discussing here, of course, is the application in the field of international relations in the society of states of some of the general principles of conflict which were outlined in earlier chapters. On the one hand we have to note the way in which conflicts escalate to the point of mutual destruction by the more violent means (and, of course, in the case of relations between states those most violent means play a more prominent part). On the other we have to consider what happens with the de-escalation of conflict, the restoration of peace and the establishment of a new order.

A nation state, being a compulsory association, is more capable of collective action than any other group. We have seen, however, as the argument has developed, that this unity is itself less than perfect and that one of the ways of prosecuting a conflict is to play upon the divisions and conflicts which exist in the enemy's society or in a more complex process in the society of third parties. We must now turn to these internal divisions and conflicts.

Civil War

The notion of civil war involves the recognition that the kinds of conflict which we have been discussing occur not merely between nation states, but within them. We speak of civil war when the parties to any conflict are prepared to prosecute that conflict by violent means and by so doing deny what is of the essence of the definition of the state, namely its monopoly of the legitimate means of physical coercion.[1]

Civil war, however, implies the existence of conflict groups which pursue their conflicts by other means. Such groups, unlike the nation state, are not compulsory associations and their very existence and capacity for collective action must be taken as problematic. We must now consider, therefore, the meaning of conflict between nations without states, ethnic groups and classes.

Nations without states

It is obvious that there still do exist certain nations in the world which do not possess the attributes of sovereignty or, to put it another way, do not have a state. Although the Wilsonian dispensation of 1919 required the recognition of the principle of rational self-determination, that principle was only imperfectly realised even in Europe. The government of Great Britain, for example, was located in England and claimed to speak and act on behalf of the peoples of England, Wales, Scotland and Northern Ireland. The Basques were incorporated in Spain and

France. Belgium remained an irredeemably plural society with power precariously shared by the Flemish and Walloon people. Countries like Yugoslavia were essentially federations of nationalities. It could be argued that the Wilsonian dispensation required that in the future there would be more smaller nation states and that there was likely to be prolonged conflict between these submerged nations and their nation states before this goal was achieved.[2]

But what exactly is a nation without a state? Does the notion imply that such nations did historically possess sovereignty? Or is the term to be applied to a group which, because of distinct cultural, religious or linguistic characteristics, aspires to be a sovereign entity? In any case what does it mean to speak of a group having characteristics? In a non-compulsory association, how far do all the individuals thought of as members have the relevant characteristics?

Suppose that one is dealing with a minority group within a sovereign state whose members are thought of as having a different religion and language from the majority of the population. Not all 'members' will in fact have the supposed characteristics. Some will have adopted the majority religion or relapsed into secularism. They may not even speak the national language or they may be bilingual. And even if they have the characteristics of possessing the minority religion and speaking its own language they may still feel loyal to the nation state within which their 'nation' is situated.

The mobilization of a rebel nation

Nations, in this sense, only exist to the extent to which they have been mobilised. The entity, the nation, is something which is posited and brought into being by ideologists.[3] It is not a given sociological fact. Once it exists ideologically, however, the idea of the nation becomes a potential focus of loyalty. A core of committed members develop and a much wider group who feel a sense of belonging, or at least passively acquiesce, to the idea of this separate national identity.

Separate nationhood within the nation state is essentially a treasonable idea. Those who preach it call on their fellows to deny their loyalty to the nation state and to put loyalty to their own more intimate nation first. This creates a drama of rebellion and the individuals who perform that first drama become the core members of the new nation. They will consist of individuals who are prepared to act and not merely to speak. To raise the flag of rebellion effectively they have to be prepared to take part in acts such as assassination and sabotage.

To describe the nation without a state in these terms is to draw attention to the obverse fact, that there are many for whom the core members claim to speak who regard those core members as 'extremists' either in their goals or in the means which they use. But a nation achieves a separate identity in so far as there is a sufficient number of those for whom these extremists claim to speak, who at least acquiesce in support for their cause. The number of these may well increase if the government 'over-reacts' to the acts of terrorism of the core members.

Governments will react to national independence movements partly by repression and partly by proposing compromise solutions. The devolution of some authority and the recognition of the right of the separate nation to conduct some of its own affairs, particularly cultural affairs, will be a common tactic. As against this the nationalist leaders will seek political, economic and military independence. After devolution the struggle will continue.

Nationalist and class struggle

A very important factor in the conflict of loyalties between the suppressed nation and the inclusive state will be the extent to which commitment is affected by material interests. Many left-wing nationalists have seen the bourgeoisie of their own group as 'selling out' to the state in return for positions and income. In fact, however, the reverse may also be the case. A rational bourgeoisie might see more hopes for themselves through separation than they can have as a subordinate part of the bourgeoisie of a unified state. So far as the working class is concerned it is quite likely, if there is a situation of 'internal colonialism', that their class struggle will be a struggle for separation. Therefore, a separatist movement may well contain both right- and left-wing bourgeois and working-class elements.

Here we begin to see the coincidence of class struggles and national independence struggles and this is a theme to which we shall be forced to return when we discuss the case of class conflict in a capitalist society. Before we do this we must discuss the special case of internal nationalism to be found in the colonial plural society.

The plural society debate

The theory of the colonial plural society as a separate part of sociological theorising owes its origins to J. S. Furnivall.[4] Furnivall saw a colonial society as being held together, so far as inter-ethnic ties were concerned, primarily by the market-place. The exchange relations of the market-place tended to be particularly harsh and exploitative because they were not embedded in any moral order, such as had prevailed with the development of capitalism in Europe. The moral bonding of colonial society was to be found solely within the separate ethnic groups.

This formulation of the plural society concept did not of itself lead to a theory of conflict, except in so far as exchange theory implies conflict theory. Nor is there a conflict theory contained in the formulation of M. G. Smith.[5] Smith uses Malinowski's account of a socio-cultural system in describing the institutional structure of the separate ethnic groups in a plural society, claiming that each group has a nearly complete set of institutions within itself, lacking only the political institution. A feature of such societies is that they are held together by political domination. We can, indeed, only speak of a society in these terms if one of the plural ethnic groups succeeds in dominating the others politically. After the withdrawal of a colonial power such societies are likely to break up unless one of the ethnic segments takes over the dominating role.

Furnivall emphasises economic ties divorced from a normative context. Smith emphasises political ties in a similar way. Neither develops a theory of conflict, but neither are they functionalists. Together they focus attention on the political and economic ties between groups within which it is clear that conflict is likely to occur. The groups confront one another in a market-place armed with political power and divorced from any concept of moral obligation or a normative order. In such circumstances a process of class struggle which is also a political struggle is bound to ensue.

Elsewhere I have criticised M. G. Smith[6] for not recognising that the various ethnic groups within his system perform economic functions and that those economic functions continue after political independence, but it is also true that the economic bonds between groups also produce class struggle. The ethnically plural society is a class society and the class struggle in colonial society often takes an ethnic form.

A relative truce in the ethnic class struggle is often achieved in post-colonial society through the separate elements forming a symbiotic relationship with one another, especially when one of the ethnic segments plays a predominantly economic role and the other a political one. This seems to be the situation in territories like Malaysia. There is, however, no finality in this. A younger generation of Chinese in Malaysia may seek to share in political power and a younger generation of Malays to enter business. When such challenges occur men defend their power and their property, and open and violent conflict ensues. Another possibility in the post-colonial situations is that alien groups who have enjoyed a monopoly of the lesser economic functions during colonialism will no longer be tolerated and will become the target of persecution and expulsion.

That inter-group conflict of this sort should occur in colonial and post-colonial society is understandable. The groups concerned were originally separate nations or parts of separate nations and were brought together as a result of the colonial conquest of one nation (or nations) by another. Group formation for purposes of political and economic conflict therefore needs no special explanation. The groups are there already. Given the development of a new pattern of conflicting interests they are available as collective actors.

The problematic concept of class conflict

What we have been discussing so far, in fact, are situations in which clearly demarcated and mobilised groups engage in conflict. On the one hand we spoke of nation states; on the other of groups bound together by primordial *Gemeinschaft* ties of language, kinship, religion and common history. Strangely enough, however, it is not groups of this kind which have preoccupied conflict theorists. Under the influence of Marx they have taken class conflict as normal and have regarded allegiance to ethnic and national groupings as problematic, to be explained in terms of false consciousness. We shall now reverse this procedure, taking national and ethnic groups as given and regarding classes as problematic. In this way we shall show that class can be a useful sociological concept of some centrality in the sociology of conflict.

We have already used the concept of class in this sense in Chapter 2, on markets and conflict. There we saw that free markets give way to collective bargaining and that as collective bargaining broke down into open conflict, groups were formed of more or less cohesiveness, depending upon such factors as the strength of interests involved, leadership skill and effectiveness of organisation. Obviously, when the group involved already had the solidarity of a closed natural group there would be little need for these factors to operate. It is in their absence that the other variables become important.

Class in Marx's political sociology

We must now look at the way in which the notion of class is used by Karl Marx. His usage is in fact a very rich one and has shaped the political thought of Europe for the past century. Precisely for that reason, however, we need to look analytically at the way the concept is used in order to show its relation to the kinds of concepts which have been developed here. In so far as it goes beyond and improves on those concepts we should be able to clarify exactly what is being claimed.

The key writings of Marx are those written between 1847 and 1852. This was the period in which he was escaping from a Hegelian problematic and a Hegelian style of thought into an overtly political sociology. After this period he was inclined to take class struggle for granted, but to deal with the logically prior problem of the development of a labour market, which bourgeois economists regarded as a natural phenomenon, but which he saw as concealing a primal act of exploitation. In following through and demystifying the explanation of bourgeois economics he did not again turn to the creation of the collective actors who would engage in revolutionary political combat. It is therefore to the political writings that we must now turn.

In the earlier Hegelian writings Marx had been primarily concerned with philosophical questions relating to the overcoming of alienation. He saw labour rather than thought as the means of overcoming alienation and therefore assigned a primary role to the proletariat in his philosophy of history.[7] As against Hess and the True Socialists he saw the proletariat as being the agent which would usher in the new age of socialism.

By 1847, however, Marx is impatient with Hegelian conceptualisation and when he deals with the particularly crass use of these concepts by Proudhon he himself uses them ironically, but in so doing suggests a wholly new problematic. Thus he takes up the Hegelian distinction between things-in-themselves and things-for-themselves and applies them to social classes. In a famous passage he writes:

Economic conditions had first transformed the mass of the people of the country into workers. The combination of capital has created for this mass a common situation, common interests. This mass is thus already a class as against capital, but not yet for itself. In the struggle, of which we have noted only a few phases, this mass becomes united, and constitutes itself as a class-for-itself. The interests it defends become class interests. But the struggle of class against class is a political struggle.

Here then is an important distinction between two stages of class formation. A class-in-itself is produced by 'economic conditions', but this becomes a class-for-itself in the course of political struggle. What is the sociological meaning of this distinction?

A first distinction is being made between unconsciousness and consciousness or, in more complex terms, between true and false consciousness. The workers at the lowest level of all might be thought of as nearly unconscious, as responding automatically to their masters' will. At a slightly more conscious level they might be able to give reasons why they should obey; that is they might regard the rule of their masters as legitimate. Thirdly, they might see their relations with their masters as market relations only.

This third stage of consciousness is one of very considerable sociological significance, for once social relations are viewed in this way, we pass from a basically moral and political ordering of society to one based upon the market. It might have been expected then that Marx would have regarded this stage as the emergence of a class-for-itself. The fact, however, is that he does not. He is not merely concerned with the breaking-out from traditional types of domination and legitimate order, but much more with breaking-out of the order imposed by bourgeois ideology. It is through the market and its rationalisation in the laws of economics that bourgeois domination is maintained. To understand the 'true' position of the worker we have to turn from economics to political theory or from the economics of marginal utility to the theory of social conflict.

This, however, in no way conflicts with what we have said in our own analysis of conflict and market situations. What we saw there was that market bargaining was one way, and only a temporary way at that, of resolving conflicts. In the long run, monopoly on both sides of the bargaining process forces the parties into two-sided conflict. Thus the 'political struggle' to which Marx refers is immanent in the market situation itself. We would only wish to add, in the light of what has already been said in this chapter, that the recognition of even a market-bargaining situation involves a significant sociological step beyond the primordial solidarity of master and servant.

It would seem, in fact, that there are three stages which we can envisage in the relations between master and servant or employer and employee. There is the stage in which they are held together by the bonds of tradition, by political domination and by shared concepts of political authority. There is the stage in which they see themselves as engaged in buying or selling labour at a price. Finally, there is the stage in which they see themselves as engaged in conflict where no concept of legitimate authority prevents the use of more drastic sanctions than the market allows.

It is of some interest here to refer back to the concepts used by Furnivall. He sees the market relations *between* ethnic groups in colonial society as different from those in the advanced industrial countries in that market relations are not embedded in a normative order. While this could mean that he sees the latter situation as one in which the market is still contained and limited within the moral order, it could also mean that he sees the colonial situation as one in which the second stage of market relations is by-passed and that 'the struggle' is always a 'political struggle'.

The mobilization of classes

It should now be noticed, however, that political struggle is not something which occurs automatically between collective actors. The collective actors have to be formed and mobilised so that the individuals who are their members feel sufficient allegiance to them to put their commitment to this new grouping before all others. This is to say that they must not be apathetic, that they must be prepared to renounce all prior loyalties and that they must even put their loyalty to the class or conflict group before their loyalty to the state.

The process of class formation which makes possible the supersession of other ties appears to involve three elements. These are leadership and organisation, the creation of an internal normative order within the class and the emergence of group identification or we-feeling. These may be illustrated in the case of the traditional working class in Great Britain.

A core of organisations of a purely associational sort is provided in deliberately created organisations like trade unions. Members of such organisations actually hold cards and some are appointed as leaders, officers and representatives. Unions, however, themselves rely upon a wider support from non-members who identify with their cause, and when other than industrial issues arise a wider labour movement comes into existence in which there are, strictly speaking, no members, but in which a sufficient number of individuals recognise a common leadership and unite for purposes of collective action. Obviously the existence of this wider labour movement is a matter of more or less at particular times and places.

A very important question concerns the way in which the solidarity achieved through trade union organisation is extended to the wider movement within which there is no formal membership. Parties are important here. They are, of course, also formal organisations; but they deliberately attempt, through electoral and other forms of political mobilisation, to unite followers and supporters far beyond the range of their formal membership. Lenin explored one sociological possibility with his notion of the disciplined vanguard party which: (a) had tightly organised and disciplined membership; (b) required of its members a total commitment and loyalty excluding or subordinating all others; and (c) had an evangelistic and teaching role for the members of the class beyond the party. He believed that only trade union consciousness (and he might have said trade union organisation) was spontaneous and that a wider political consciousness depended upon the establishment of a party which would command authority over the class as a whole. In parliamentary democracies where the Leninist model does not prevail, parties of the working class use elections and the opportunities which they give for teaching to mobilise the masses behind common programmes.

Unity behind programmes and teachers, however, is not sufficient to give long-term unity to a class. Ideally it must establish its own cultural and moral order which unites members with one another and cuts them off from a wider society. It is the existence of an order of this kind which has helped to give strength to the working class in Britain and other European countries.

Richard Hoggart[8] is one of those who have drawn attention to the distinctiveness of working-class culture on this level. He, however, gives attention primarily to the norms of domestic and communal life. What is important is that the norms which he describes are extended to, and gain strength from, their role in the world of work. That is to say they are class norms and not merely the norms of the traditional *Gemeinschaft*.

The solidarity of the working class which derives from its norms is threatened in two ways. One is that they should become subordinated to the norms of the local or regional *Gemeinschaft*. The other is that they will become undermined by the individualism of bourgeois society at large. Hoggart's work is uniquely interesting in its detailed analysis of the way in which the latter process works.

The third aspect of class unity is the growth of group identification and we-feeling. It is still a remarkable feature of British society that this does exist for large numbers of people. They say 'I'm working class' meaning that their self-concept is tied up with the notion of class and' that this identity is one which, for most of the time at least, takes priority over others.

What we are saying here is that in some of the older industrial countries like Britain there are a sufficient number of people who respond to working-class leadership, who share a common culture and have a class-based identity for us to speak of the existence of a working class. But we must now ask, 'Is this what Marx meant by a class-in-itself or does that term have to be restricted more narrowly?'

Marx's ideal type of class mobilization

There can be little doubt that Marx did mean more than this and that the traditional working class in Britain would have seemed to him to fall short of being a class-for-itself. Clearly, we too would have to recognise that the sort of collective organisation and solidarity which we have outlined above belongs not merely under the heading of conflict-group formation but also under the heading of status-based and traditionally based community.

None the less it is important from the point of view of the sociology of conflict not to dismiss this kind of class situation as irrelevant. What has happened after all is that instead of a simple situation in which there are a number of sub-cultures related to status groups and regions, we now have groups which engage at least in collective bargaining with each other and whose normative order and group identity is affected by this fact. We are not dealing with groups which are related to each other co-operatively or symbiotically but groups related by conflict. It is a significant fact about a society if a large part of its population are affected by such groupings. Most usually the ties of class cannot compete with the primordial ties of community on the one hand or the individualising forces of the market on the other.

Marx, however, reserved the term 'class-for-itself' not merely for the 'two warring camps' which he saw as more and more evident under capitalism, but for a much more specific case. This was the case in which an exploited or oppressed class sought not merely to defend itself within the system, but in which it sought hegemony and attempted to overthrow the existing system. Clearly, this too is a theoretically important case even if it has no empirical exemplification in the history of capitalist class formation.

In fact it was this notion of the class as a group seeking hegemony which played a large part in Marx's thinking about political revolution. Thus, while on the one hand there is a theory of classes forming in the labour market and organising in order to take more and more effective action, on the other there is the notion of an oppressed and exploited class becoming mobilised to fight not merely to defend itself but to establish its own social and cultural order on all men. It is this notion which plays the most important role in the *Communist Manifesto*.

The *Communist Manifesto* begins with a thumb-nail sociological sketch of the history of the bourgeoisie as a class and, having described the now completed process by which the bourgeoisie has attained hegemony, goes on to suggest that 'a similar movement is going on before our very eyes', which will lead to the formation of the proletariat as a class and, in the long run, to proletarian hegemony.

The history of the bourgeoisie goes through a number of sharply defined sociological stages. First, there is the stage in which their progenitors are nothing more than a band of outlaws. Second, there is the stage in which they are an armed and independent estate. Thirdly, there is the stage in which the internal cultural order of the class is transformed. Finally, there is the stage in which it imposes its hegemony on society as a whole and transforms all social relations and all cultural norms so that they accord with its own.

The first stage here is that of a break with the traditional order. The bourgeoisie are a 'band of outlaws', i.e. are outside the law of medieval society. This does not, however, mean that they are lawless. They develop their own law and customs and morality around the notion of exchange and profit in opposition to the law of medieval society based upon notions such as authority and mutual aid.

The second stage is the stage of becoming an armed and independent estate. Since it was in the nature of medieval European society that there was no strong centralised state, it was possible for a new society to grow up within that society with its own separate military power and its own distinctive cultural order. Such a development would obviously be less likely in a unitary society with a strong centralised state.

In the third stage we see the full development of bourgeois social relations. Within the 'armed and independent estate' there were no doubt a number of different factors making for solidarity. What is now worked out, however, is a social order based upon the 'callous cash nexus'.

It does not, however, suffice for the bourgeoisie that it should transform its own internal culture, its own internal pattern of social relations, while at the same time exploiting another class. It in effect abolishes all other classes by imposing its own pattern of social relations upon them. It does not simply exploit the labour of others as earlier classes have done. It exploits labour itself as a commodity. The whole social world is organised as a set of market-places.

When Marx speaks of 'a similar movement going on before our very eyes' it is clear that he believes that there will be a rough correspondence between these four stages in the history of the bourgeoisie and four stages in the history of the proletariat. That is to say, the proletariat starts its life as a class outside of the estate system of pre-revolutionary France; it challenges the existing order sufficiently to become a law unto itself; it develops its own internal cultural order and patterning of social relations sharply distinct from that of the bourgeois order; and eventually it will establish its own 'social and economic sway' based upon these new social relations.

But Marx is not content merely to indicate such a rough parallelism. The proletariat has its own characteristic stages of development. The earliest stage perhaps was still that described in metaphysical terms in the *Critique of Hegel's Philosophy of Right*. It is 'a class which is the dissolution of all classes, a sphere of society which has a universal character because its sufferings are universal and which does not claim a particular redress, because the wrong done to it is not a particular wrong, but wrong in general'.[9]

At this stage the proletariat has no stake of its own in society.

But what the *Communist Manifesto* goes on to describe is precisely the organisation of the proletariat as a class within society.

At first the fight is not directed at the proletariat's enemies, but at the enemies of its enemies. The capitalists themselves organise their workers to fight against the remnants of the old order. But, in doing this, they provide them with weapons which will be used against themselves.

From fighting for the Reform Bill, the British working class went on to fight for its own interests. This was done in the first place through the trade unions, which, having access to modern transport very quickly went on to become national associations. The unions in turn would give birth to a political party which would act on behalf of the class to create a new social order. Strangely, however, the *Manifesto* does not carry through the story of this party's thrust to hegemony and stops short with only a moderate reformist programme. Undoubtedly Marx believed that once the party succeeded in exerting its power in support of this programme it would gradually manoeuvre itself into a position from which it could undermine bourgeois society as a whole.

Alternative possible outcomes in the class struggle

I have suggested elsewhere[10] that in any conflict situation between two classes, parties or political parties, there are three possible outcomes, which I called the ruling-class situation, the truce situation and the revolutionary situation. In the first the ruling class or group succeeded in establishing its own institutions against the attempt of those it ruled to set up their own counter-institutions. In the second a partial modification of the institutional order of the ruling class was attained through the concession of some of the demands of the ruled (as for instance in the case of welfare states under capitalism). In the third case the oppressed or exploited group was in a position to establish its own order, but might well find that its way of life, designed for defence in the days of struggle, could not be extended to the whole society.

Some such modification of the Marxian model of class struggle in a capitalist society appears to be necessary since it is not always the case that the proletariat is able to organise itself as a separate class, let alone an 'armed and independent estate'; it has very often wrung concessions from the bourgeoisie so as to establish, at least for long periods, a truce situation; and, finally, when it has been in a position to establish its own hegemony, it has not been able to draw on its own internal order for a model for society as a whole. All of these possibilities must be recognised in the sociology of conflict.

Primordial ties and ties of economic interest

A prior point should, however, be considered in relation to the Marxian account of the sociology of conflict. We have in the earlier part of this chapter considered the role of compulsory associations and of groups based upon primordial ties in the development of conflict. By contrast with these, Marx's notion of conflict between classes differentiated in terms of their members' relationship to the means of production requires some justification. Whereas the other types of grouping presuppose a man already enmeshed in social ties, the Marxian classes and, indeed, the groups which we discussed in Chapter 2, are assumed to arise from a coincidence of interests between individual men. The question is whether this assumption is ever realistic. Whereas many Marxists claim that allegiance to groups other than classes represents false consciousness, an argument can be put that whereas the other forms of consciousness which we have discussed are natural the purported rational bonds of class are artificial. In Tönnies'[11] terms, classes are associations not communities.

As a general theory of social differentiation applying to all societies, Marxism might even more readily be questioned. Marxism proposes the development of differentiation within a society amongst men formerly related to one another. The state is then seen as a means whereby one class dominates another. For Franz Oppenheimer,[12] on the other hand, the state is always and everywhere the product of conquest. The differentiation within the group governed by the state is essentially the differentiation between originally separate groups – the conquerors and the conquered.

The relative disappearance of primordial ties in bourgeois society There is undoubtedly some truth in Oppenheimer's approach. Moreover, it has the merit of seeing the phenomenon of the plural society which is so problematic for Marxists as the normal case. But we may still question Oppenheimer's theory as being of universal application. In particular we might question its applicability to bourgeois society. For it is the unique feature of bourgeois society that it undermines all pre-existing ties. This is what is meant in one of the more lyrical passages in the *Communist Manifesto*:

> The bourgeoisie, wherever it has got the upper hand, has put an end to all feudal, patriarchal, idyllic relations. It has pitilessly torn asunder the motley feudal ties that bound man to his 'natural superiors' and has left remaining no other nexus between man and man than callous 'cash payment'. It has drowned the most heavenly ecstasies of religious fervour, of philistine sentimentalism in the icy water of egotistical calculation. It has resolved personal worth into exchange value and in place of the numberless indefensible chartered freedoms has set up that single unconscionable freedom – Free Trade. In one word, for exploitation, veiled by religious and political illusions, it has substituted naked shameless direct brutal exploitation.[13]

The bourgeois revolution thus ushers in a whole new sociological era based upon rational calculation and the abolition of primordial ties. In the circumstances, the proletariat in part resists the new order, clinging to its regional cultural ties, but in part adjusts to it, forming its own associational class for the pursuit of conflict.

In so far as the proletariat breaks with its primordial ties and becomes an associational class it is on the way to becoming fully conscious in Marxian terms or becoming a class-for-itself. When this happens one is likely to see the subsequent development of conflict along the lines which we have suggested in Chapter 2.

Non-economic factors in modern political conflict

There are, however, other possibilities, both when the proletariat does not develop along these lines or when the conflict which divides a society does not appear to be a market-based one at all. We are now in a position to review some of these other principles.

Internal conflicts within any society often turn upon a threat to the primordial ties existing within groups. These include ties of common religion and language in particular. The conflict may simply reflect the continuance of an old conflict which existed before the group were united in one state or might turn upon new cultural developments. If the latter is the case it is quite possible that the new developments are themselves the result of transformation in the economic sphere. The people with their traditional religion may be confronted with the bourgeoisie in the guise of Protestants, as the Weber thesis suggests, or may resist the new order in the name of religion.[14] Similarly, secular radical parties which confront clericalism may often represent nothing other than the secularism of the bourgeoisie.

Whether conflicts of this kind are conflicts with an ascendant bourgeoisie or not, however, it must be noted that in their development the goals sought by the parties are not simply material ones, but very often the right to use a language or worship in a particular way. The parties will seek to defeat and suppress the competing language or religion by banning its dissemination through schools and churches, or at least to achieve a compromise in which alternative patterns are allowed to coexist segregated from one another.

It is a matter of judgement, however, whether a particular conflict can be settled purely on the cultural level. In the case of the Six Counties of Northern Ireland, for example, a mere religious settlement would in no way end a conflict whose roots are to be found in international conflict and in competing economic systems.

Power conflict as class conflict

Very different from conflicts of the kind which we have been discussing, are conflicts over power and authority as suggested in the Dahrendorf thesis.[15] These arise not out of factors surviving from the pre-bourgeois era but from developments within it.

We cannot accept the provocative Dahrendorf thesis that conflicts over power are the fundamental social process and that market conflicts of the kind discussed by Marx are only a special case of the more general type. In so far as they are market conflicts they do not involve the element of authority which exists in other cases. It is true that labour markets exist within the context of social organisations structured on the basis of authority, but, in so far as market bargaining operates at all, such authority is held at least temporarily in abeyance.

What is important about the power-class thesis is its recognition (a) that market bargaining breaks down into a power struggle, and (b) that one possible outcome of such a struggle is the introduction of bureaucratic allocation instead of market allocation of resources. So far as (a) is concerned our own theory outlined in Chapter 2 requires no amendment and Marx, too, might claim that he was well aware that a class-in-itself only became a class-for-itself in the course of a political struggle. More significant, however, is the question of bureaucratic allocation.

The fact that bureaucratic allocation involves a step in the direction of substantive rationality (i.e. the substitution of precise goals for the 'utility' of the separate participants) does not mean that group conflict ceases. The question now becomes one of whose goals are to be pursued. Whereas the Marxian class struggle took place between groups differentiated in terms of their relation to the means of production, now conflict occurs between groups differentiated in terms of their relation to the political apparatus. The history of the Soviet Union certainly seems to suggest that under socialism such group differentiation continues to exist. This is one aspect of the Dahrendorf thesis that remains of continuing significance. It would be unfortunate if it were pursued in a purely ideological way to score points against socialism by showing that it was no better than capitalism. What would be more interesting would be an empirical attempt to chart and then to analyse the kinds of conflict which exist under a centrally planned economic regime.

Some of the conflicts which continue in socialist countries are those with national and religious minorities. These are not particularly important, because they are simply a new version of the struggle between rationalistic and primordial ties which exist in bourgeois society, even if new and often insecure socialist regimes find them a little more difficult to tolerate. More important are the conflicts between groups differentially placed in relation to the means of production which continue as these groups struggle to influence the planning apparatus. If primordial groups represent a double survival into bourgeois and socialist society, groups differentially placed in relation to the means of production represent at least a single survival into socialism.

The continued existence of groups of this kind gives support not so much to the Dahrendorf as the Burnham thesis.[16] Ownership of the means of production may be abolished but the distinction between control and non-control or between differing degrees of control still exists. But these are still classes in relation to the means of production and not power classes. The question in a socialist society may well be which of these classes has access to the political apparatus. The claim of the Soviet government is that it acts for the proletariat, but the evidence which can be derived from the origins of the surviving leadership in the fifty years since the revolution[17] suggests that managerial groups may have captured control of the apparatus.

On the other hand it must also be pointed out that the party apparatus in the Soviet Union also subverts class formation. A plant manager may find that he cannot get his will carried out because the party, represented amongst both workers and management, decides otherwise. If this process were completely carried through one would have the abolition of classes in relation to the means of production and the crucial group struggles would go on between groups differentiated solely in terms of their relationship to the political apparatus.

Class conflict and immigrant labour

One other development has to be located within the sociology of capitalist and socialist rather than traditional society. This is the conflict between immigrant labour, native-born labour, employers and governments in the advanced industrial societies. In all such societies the established labour force will have made some gains, will have usurped authority[18] from the employers and the ruling class and will have succeeded in establishing some substantively rational goals for the economy, particularly in the form of the recognition of minimum standards of welfare. The question then becomes whether the newly won rights are regarded as applying to all or only to members of the organised usurping class. In so far as they only apply to the latter, the immigrant workforce finds itself in the position of an underclass.

Myrdal[19] has suggested that this term should be applied to a hopeless and despairing mass who have dropped out of the competitive system or the class system. I have suggested in my own work on colonial immigrants in Britain[20] that such immigrants may become not merely an underclass but an 'underclass-for-itself', a third party to the class struggle. Whether this separation and the struggle between underclass and working class is only a temporary phase remains to be seen. One thing, however, is clear. The conflict which does occur is not simply an ethnic, cultural or racial one. Ethnic bonds may strengthen the capacity of such groups to become an underclass-for-itself, but they are not the sole source of the underclass's origin. What is far more important is the connection which such an immigrant class establishes between the developed and underdeveloped or colonial social systems and economies.

Conclusion: classes and other collective actors

In this chapter we have reversed the normal Marxist-inspired tendency to see primordial non-economic ties as representing false consciousness only. We began with the compulsory ties of nationhood and the primordial ties of ethnicity. What we have sought to show, however, is that with the bourgeois disenchantment of the world new processes are set in train which compete with, and often transcend, these more traditional ties. Marxism has provided us with a line of argument for elucidating in ideal-typical fashion the nature of purely associational class formations. We have shown, however, both that such associational classes have to compete with older social bonds and that the class struggle initiated by the bourgeois revolution may well continue in new forms, even after bourgeois society has been modified or transcended by the political victories of the working class and of the imposition of the principle of substantive rationality on the economy.

5

A PARADIGM FOR CONFLICT ANALYSIS

The relative primacy of order and conflict in sociological theory

Talcott Parsons claimed that the central problem of sociological theory was the 'problem of order'. In fact it could be said that he addressed himself to the 'problem of conflict'. Order in *The Social System* was taken to be a necessary condition of life and much of the book was addressed to the ways in which the mechanisms for producing order went to work on incipient conflicts and eliminated them.

One way of reconciling structuralist–functionalist order theory and conflict theory is simply to suggest that they apply in different situations. There are some social systems and social structures, it is argued, which are orderly and stable and others which are ridden with conflict and unstable. In the former case structural–functional theory is thought to be appropriate and, in the latter, conflict theory.

Obviously some such division of labour does occur in sociology, even if it means that there will be a problem of choice as to which theory to apply and the possibility that sociology will be either ideological and conservative, *promoting* stability by emphasising it in the analysis, or Utopian and radical, promoting change. Not surprisingly, therefore, the claim is made for both structural functionalism and conflict theory that the one is more basic than the other and more in accord with the scientific truth.

Which of these positions is adopted will turn ultimately on the question of the relation between power and the normative order. In Parsons' work[1] the normative order is taken as given, as the ultimate determinant of the social system, and power is therefore conceived as a resource to be put in the hands of role-players who are working to achieve systemic goals. The other alternative is to reject the idea of normative consensus, to assume that different parties have different goals and to argue that any particular *status quo* rests upon the resultant of clashing forces or powers. In this second case norms are dependent, to be functionally explained as necessary given a particular power balance.

The claim which we are making here is that the second sort of theory is the most fundamental in sociology. Whether or not a given situation is orderly, the norms which are in operation must be understood in relation to the underlying social balance of power, which is the most fundamental social fact. This is a position which is sometimes thought of as 'materialist' as compared with the idealism of theories like Parsons'. In fact, however, this is misleading if materialism is identified with Marxism, since in Marx's work neither norms nor power, but creative labour, has primacy. The view advocated here owes more to Hobbes or Machiavelli than Marx and, in sociology, to Simmel and Weber. It is perhaps not surprising that contemporary Marxism and functionalism have much in common. Both emphasise social systems. In conflict theory systems are secondary, to be understood in terms of more fundamental concepts of purposive and instrumental action.

Parsons, of course, rejects the possibility that the ends of individuals are simply random from the point of view of the social system. We would not wish to maintain in opposition to this that ends are purely individual. In any ongoing historical society the ends which men seek are culturally conditioned and men do form alliances to pursue shared goals. But this is by no means to suggest, as Parsons does, that men orient their action to values which by happy coincidence serve also to integrate the collectivity.[2]

It should also be noted that Parsons makes the accusation of treating ends as random from the point of view of the system, not at conflict theory but at the whole utilitarian tradition, including all economic theory. Now while it is true that utilitarianism, economic theory and exchange theory are all to be understood as opposed to structural functionalism on this point, there are none the less fundamental differences between exchange theory and conflict theory.

The whole point about exchange theory which is essentially an attempt to base sociological theory on the theory of economics is that, although it starts by assuming actors who have conflicting goals, it posits the possibility of a point being reached at which each individual pursues his own ends in a way which is actually beneficial to the other. Although it starts with the potentiality of conflict it ends with what is in effect a process of co-operation.

Conflict theory approaches this problem from the opposite side. It starts with what appears to be a mutually beneficial exchange, but discovers within this relation elements of compulsion and exploitation which appear as normative only because the oppressed and the exploited do not have the power to resist them. It then focusses on the power underlying the relationship and considers the consequences of a change in the balance of power.

A further element also distinguishes conflict theory from exchange theory when the latter is extended to constitute a theory of market behaviour. The peacefulness of the market, as we have seen in Chapter 2, rests upon the use of the sanction of 'going to another supplier'. This peaceful process, however, is seen to break down in economic theory, and the theory of the free market has to be supplemented by a theory of oligopoly and monopoly. What is an embarrassment for exchange theory and economic theory, however is the essence of the matter for conflict theory. Market sanctions (i.e. the sanction of 'going to another supplier') are used to regulate particular transactions only because there is the possibility of resort to the more fundamental political conflict if there is monopoly on both sides of the market. They represent a convenient way of solving particular problems within a fundamentally political order which rests upon a balance of power.

A last general point to be made is that conflict theory does not imply a reduction of society to a war of each individual against every other individual all of the time. Conflict does not mean random disorder. It must allow for the formation of collectivities in pursuit of conflict and it assumes functional interconnectedness between institutional areas so that conflicts in one area are sustained and supported by conflicts in others.

The range and application of conflict theory

With these points made we may turn to the task of setting out systematically the main points of conflict analysis as a systematic approach to the study of the social.

1. *The nature of the unit to be studied*

Clearly, conflict theory can be applied at various levels. It can be applied in individual dyadic relations and in large-scale relations between collectivities such as classes and nations. However, the move from relations between individuals to that between collectivities implies a theory of collective mobilisation since that is itself a variable and a sanction in the conflict situation.

2. *The nature of the conflict process involved*

The dyadic conflict relation is only the simplest case of social conflict, whether between individuals or collectivities. In this simple case there are no third parties and the conflict is thought of as being fought out on one institutional level. Obviously, however, many conflict situations grow out of multi-party situations like markets, and the conflict which in its rawest form is a power struggle involving the threat of physical violence may be pursued in a variety of interrelated institutional contexts.

3. *Dyadic conflict of a micro-sociological kind*

Clearly, the problem with which a sociologist may be confronted may be one of a purely interpersonal kind, e.g. the struggle between two individuals seeking to exercise their wills within an organisation or a marital relationship. In all such cases one has to look at the following elements:

(a) the goals of the two parties;
(b) their consequent expectations of one another;
(c) the degree of understanding which they have of each other's expectations;

(d) their motivation to conform with expectations either because of (1) self-interest or (2) acceptance of a normative order or (3) emotional ties with each other;

(e) in the case of there being a normative order, motivation to comply with it or to deviate;

(f) the sanctions available to, and employed by, the parties to realise their wills against those of opponents; and

(g) the capacities of the parties to pursue the conflict.

Finally, since all of these elements are considered in relation to a rational–calculating attitude to the situation seen in the light of goals desired, one would need to look at the possibility of the action of the parties deviating from the rational because of disturbances on the level of the personality system and the operation of various psychological mechanisms. Some theories of conflict, including that of Parsons,[3] are inclined to assimilate all conflicts to this model, thus reducing it to a kind of psychological deviance. We certainly do not intend this, but we would not wish to exclude the possibility that some conflicts are purely of this sort and that to some extent all conflict situations are complicated by affective and non-rational elements.

The two examples of conflicts of a dyadic interpersonal kind which we suggest in order to illustrate the use of this theoretical analysis are a struggle for power between two individuals in an organisation and a marital relationship.

Dyadic conflict in an organisation   In the case of a struggle for power between individuals in an organisation there is, of course, a pre-existing normative order. This, however, by no means negates the analysis of existing relations in terms of the sociology of conflict. In the first place this pre-existing normative order could itself be regarded as the outcome of a conflict within which a long-lasting truce has been negotiated. Secondly, it is possible to abstract from the present complex of normative and power relations those which are purely concerned with the struggle for power. Thirdly, in this power struggle, the normative order might be regarded either as an environment within which the power struggle is pursued or, more radically, as itself a means exploited by the parties to advance their interests.

The beginnings of the analysis of such a power struggle are in the discovery of divergent goals which the two parties are pursuing. These goals may be of a material or ideal kind. Their sustained pursuit may be the source of conflicting demands which the parties make on their situation and this itself would give rise to social conflict. What we mean by a power struggle however, is a more calculating concentration upon the intermediate goal of winning power as a generalised means to pursue goals, ideals or interests.

Once this situation has been defined the elements of our analysis will be those which we have outlined in Chapter 1. The nature of the conflict will turn first upon the degree to which expectations are fully communicated. The misunderstanding of these expectations may actually exacerbate the conflict, in that, even though a compromise on immediate issues is possible, the misunderstanding might conceal and prevent this. On the other hand, since a pure power struggle would be a zero-sum one, there could be no compromise on ultimate issues. It is therefore likely that, on the level of communication, the effect of misunderstanding might well be to diminish conflict, simply because one of the parties is unknowingly helping the other and thereby acting against his own interest.

Normative and affective factors will provide the environment within which the conflict takes place. Generally speaking, it will be less costly to accept its normative order as given and to represent any new move in the conflict as not challenging it in any way. It may even be possible to exploit it in terms of casuistical arguments showing that action along the lines intended is actually deducible from it. A third and more difficult alternative is to argue that the immediate normative order is to be suspended in accordance with norms and values of a higher order or, even more radically, to 'declare war', i.e. to posit a state in which only the most generalised norms apply. So far as affective ties are concerned, again the most effective way of pursuing the conflict may be that in which it is claimed that no affective bond is being violated at all. The formula for this would be 'I have nothing personal against you'. Alternatively, there may be a quite deliberate adoption of negative attitudes to the other. The crucial difference in its effect on the conflict would not really be whether affective attitudes are positive or negative, but, as Parsons saw clearly, whether there is ambivalence.[4] Any party who pursues a conflict ambivalently is likely to have his single-minded pursuit of goals or of power diverted into compulsive lines of conduct arising from the love–hate ambivalence which he experiences in relation to the other.

Power conflicts of this kind may well be understood as games of skill. In so far as one party plays skilfully and the other with little or no skill, the successful party should finish up possessing all the power he wishes to achieve his ends and with a minimum disturbance of the affective and normative order. A less satisfactory course would be one in which victory was won in war so that the affective order and the normative order had been at least temporarily violated and victory still required the establishment of new relations of compliance. But, as against these victorious outcomes, there is the possibility of a negotiated settlement. This might result in the sharing of power in varying proportions. At one extreme one of the parties might only have the power to be a nuisance and might therefore have to be accommodated in a small degree. At the other would be the situation in which both parties have played the best moves possible and thereby excluded any victorious outcome. In such a drawn game they might simply agree to revert to whatever was the *status quo* or agree, at least temporarily, to act as allies.

Dyadic conflict in marriage   A quite different set of constraints operates in our second example of dyadic interaction in a marital relationship. Such relationships exist within a normative and usually formally legal order, but perhaps their most unusual feature is that in Western industrial societies indeed there is a normative expectation of an ideal affective relationship in which the two parties love one another, claim to have direct inner understanding of each other's motivation and are committed to complying with each other's demands.

The actual state of play in any marriage of course falls far short of these ideals. What we actually find is an interplay between the pursuit of interests, the fulfilment of role-duties required in the legally constituted relationship and the actual dynamics of interpersonal affective relations.

If we begin in this case by looking at the goals of the parties we notice immediately that the cases in which the two parties seek only goals internal to their relations in marriage are in a small minority. The other party will himself or herself be regarded as an object of gratification both in the immediate sexual sense, but also as the source of a flow of emotional rewards. To a lesser degree, having a good marriage may be regarded as fulfilling normative requirements imposed within the larger social order.

The simplest polar case of marital disruption is that engendered by 'adultery', i.e. giving or seeking sexual and emotional gratification in other relationships and thereby devaluing the supposedly unique relation of marriage. Such action must of necessity give rise to conflict unless it is possible for both parties to accept an alternative and deviant definition of sexual and emotional relationships as not being unique.

Before we turn to the possible reactions to adultery, we should note other types of desertion which affect marriage. In the ideal Western marriage it is expected that actions of four kinds need to be accommodated. There are actions in which the parties pursue individual goals which do not disrupt the marriage. There are actions which must be pursued as the condition of existence of the marriage itself, e.g. spending thirty-five hours or so at work separated from the spouse. There are actions which the spouses pursue out of common interest and, finally, the actions which are incidental to the business of loving and making love. What has to be noted here is that marriage is not simply threatened by adultery but by the pursuit of actions which are not in accordance with an agreed balance between the different types of activity: 'work-desertion' for example is a common form of withdrawal from the marital relationship.

Withdrawal, however, is not what primarily concerns us here. We are concerned with cases in which there is a continuing marital relationship but a conflict of goals between the spouses. Such conflict occurs in all marriages, even though the idealisation of the relationship at the outset suggests that conflict is impossible. Conflict may occur over any of the four areas of action which we have mentioned when the attainment of the goals of one spouse is incompatible with the attainment of the goals of the other. It may also occur about the overall balance between the various areas as the parties deviate from one another in their conception of what the overall balance should be. ,

Obviously, whether the conflict which occurs is about the incompatibility of separate goals or incompatibility of conceptions of an ideal balance, the general pattern which we have outlined in our account of the micro-sociology of conflict applies. Conflicts may arise from misunderstanding of the other's expectations. There may be differences in the understanding of the relevant normative order. There may be a simple determination to follow incompatible goals. Moreover in this, as in every other relationship, the anchoring of the relationship in a pattern of affective ties may be threatened.

In marriage, however, this anchoring of the relationship in affective ties plays a far more fundamental role than in any other relationship, especially in the advanced industrial societies of the West where the ideal of romantic love plays so large a part. In the previous micro-sociological example which we discussed, viz. that of a struggle for power, the disturbance of affective ties was seen as an exacerbating rather than a central factor. The conflict was seen as likely to continue in an even purer form if no such disturbance occurred. In the case of marriage, however, a host of ideological considerations make it likely that any conflict is likely to be interpreted as a sign of the withdrawal of love.

Psychiatric evidence could no doubt be adduced to show that in the case of mature individuals a disturbance of the marital relation over a minor issue need not be interpreted as a threat of the withdrawal of love. Indeed it could also be argued that within love itself variation in the behaviour of the other might be regarded as tolerable and not necessarily as threatening. Much here would depend upon the socialisation of the individual and the security of the ego which results.[5] Even if this is so, however, it is clear that, given the emphasis in Western marriage on romantic love, marital conflict is likely to be readily transposed to the affective level with all the usual consequences of ambivalence, compulsive behaviour and escalating demands by parties seeking reassurance. This means that conflicts are less likely to take the form of games of skill with the possibilities which we outlined of victory for one party and the resocialisation of the vanquished or adjustment to a new balance of power. Conflicts rooted at a personality level may require therapeutic intervention if they are not to lead to extremes of violence or to breakdown of the relationship itself.

Here then are two examples of the application of the theory of conflict in a dyad where the participant actors are individuals. It is not claimed that this represents an exhaustive analysis of the conflicts involved. What we have attempted to do is merely to indicate the way in which some of the questions which arise in the micro-sociology of conflict may be asked of these relationships whether the intention is one of helping one of the parties to win or a therapeutic one of conflict resolution. We must now turn to the cases in which we are dealing not simply with a dyadic but rather with a multi-person relation, and to those cases in which the parties are not individuals but collectivities.

4. *Market relations, collective bargaining and collective conflict*

Georg Simmel[6] proceeded in his sociology from the analysis of the dyad to the analysis of more complex structures. Unfortunately he did not pursue this latter task systematically. Either he concentrated on the abstract question of the influence of numbers on social life in psychological terms or he moved to the cultural level in his account of economic life.[7] The task for a formal sociology would appear to be in the systematic elaboration of all the varieties of two-party, three-party and multi-person relations from which societies are constructed. We are not able to do this in an exhaustive way here and so concentrate on the most important of such relations, that to be found in market situations.

The market is an alternative way of providing for social needs to that which one finds in the oikos, the group, the community and the society. In these other social forms one has what Weber[8] calls budgetary management and substantively rational social provision (i.e. in which goals are deliberately chosen and appropriate means for their attainment sought or devised). In the case of markets, by contrast, one has competitive bargaining, at least a potentiality for conflict and only formal rationality (i.e. where ends are variable and rationality lies solely in the 'maximisation of utility' for the parties).

Short of a market system one has to note the case of bargaining and exchange between individuals. Here one has the simple case represented in the couplet:

The mountain sheep are sweeter, but the valley sheep are fatter,
We therefore deemed it meeter to carry off the latter.

It is, however, likely that the owner of the mountain sheep might choose an alternative course. He might explore whether or not, due to a difference of taste, the owner of the valley sheep might not be willing to exchange so that both parties gain greater satisfaction. Or, assuming that both parties value both fatness and sweetness, he might exchange some of his mountain sheep for some of the valley sheep.

Of course, getting all the valley sheep and all the mountain sheep would give the most satisfaction of all. The obstacles to this lie in the possibility of resistance by the valley man, interference by the forces of law and order or moral restraint arising from the fact that the mountain man subscribes to a moral code which he allows to govern his conduct.

There is, however, another form of pressure which the mountain man can bring. Assuming that the valley man needs sweet sheep, the mountain man may threaten to opt out of the relationship altogether and to go to another supplier for his supply of fat sheep. This may well be a more effective and less costly sanction than the resort to force.

Just as in the case of an individual bargain, however, so in this case there are two possibilities. One is that out of a complex process involving competition between fat-sheep suppliers and bargaining between sweet-sheep and fat-sheep suppliers a situation is reached in which all obtain a maximisation of their utility. The other is that it may prove more profitable to resort to force. The former is, of course, the case which is at the centre of classical economic theory. The breakdown of this simple market order is at the centre of the sociology of conflict.

There is no need to go over all the ground covered in Chapter 2 to make this point. What it is important to notice is that many needs are satisfied in society not by normatively structured group action but by bargaining and by market systems, involving bargaining and competition in combination. Here, in our paradigm for the analysis of conflict, we have to note that in any social system or structure we may find bargaining and market processes operating and that apart from those cases in which a just and satisfactory outcome is achieved for all parties, there are others in which the outcome leaves one or more parties dissatisfied or in which settlements are influenced by the use of force. We should also notice that the powerful will always be inclined to represent unjust settlements ideologically as mutually satisfactory. It is therefore necessary to explore in all cases of bargaining and market processes the underlying power situation. It may perhaps be noted here that Max Weber always combined a study of the power and property situation with the study of exchange in economics,[9] even though he accepted marginalist economics.

The sociology of conflict in fact when it is applied in this area demystifies the commodity form in precisely the way in which Marx suggested must be done in his critique of economics. However, the reality which underlies the appearance of commodities appears in the sociology of conflict not merely as the appropriation of surplus value from the worker but as a power struggle which may be the most fundamental social process of all.

But if the location of the secret of the market and the commodity form lies in the sociology of power, we should also notice the potentiality of economic theory and the sociology of conflict to doubly demystify other social relations. The selection of spouses, for instance, is represented in many sociologies as a sacred matter, or as one of the few areas left in a market-based society where the object of satisfaction has not become a commodity. Other sociologists, however, have recognised that market models might quite easily be applied to these processes and not simply to the case of prostitution in which sex is overtly for sale. This, however, still leaves the analysis at the equivalent level to that of economics, emphasising the case where all parties are satisfied in the market. The sociology of conflict goes beyond this and looks at the distribution of power and property (including for example property in good looks).

Wherever there is some possibility of applying market models, indeed there is the possibility of an analysis in terms of conflict sociology. Because of this the study of situations thought of as market situations must be listed as a quite central area in the sociology of conflict.

5. *Groups structured through market processes*

In the preceding section we drew a distinction between market structures and groups of all kinds. However, the case of the capitalist industrial firm throws some doubt upon this distinction. Although the ideological view represents such a firm as an internally co-operative enterprise in which all participants work towards the attainment of shared goals, it is in fact obvious that every basic relationship within the firm is structured in terms of markets. Capital is obtained from the capital market, raw materials are obtained in various other markets, labour is recruited in a labour market and the final product is sold in a consumer's market. Essentially the notion of an enterprise involves the attempt to relate the outcomes in all of these markets.

Marxists sometimes object to the analysis of a firm in these terms, claiming that the emphasis should be on the mode of production and not on markets. If, however, it is recognised that the markets to which we refer are not simply a means to achieve some natural equilibrium in which utility is maximised but as each involving a power struggle underlying the mystification of the commodity form, the basis for this objection largely disappears.

There is no need, however, for the conflict theorist to hold that the life of an organisation consists of nothing but a perpetual power struggle. Far from this being the case the organisation does win for itself a considerable degree of stability through truces negotiated in each of the markets. Crucially in the labour market workers agree in collective negotiations to abide by certain terms and conditions for a limited period. In these circumstances it is possible for managers to give orders and use legitimate sanctions if they are not obeyed and we should not ignore this. Equally, however, we should note that such truces are in principle temporary and will be abandoned both at the end of an agreed period and in cases where the power balance breaks down.

Dahrendorf[10] was perceptive enough to see that industrial organisations involved conflict of this sort. Indeed he went on to suggest that an analysis in these terms could be made of *any* institution or organisation. It was, however, unfortunate that he should have seen his contribution as lying in the suggestion that authority rather than property was the source of class conflict. The point is that while market bargaining is 'a special case', so is conflict about authority. In fact the market might lead to relations of authority and subordination within organisations, but the exercise of authority might be analysed in terms of bargaining and markets with all the possibilities of an outbreak of conflict which are inherent in the market. Neither property nor authority is the ultimate source of conflict. That ultimate source is to be found in power.

Dahrendorf was undoubtedly right in recognising that complete compliance with the wishes of authority was unlikely and that normally where there was authority there would also be conflict. Such conflict, however, might well be arrived at through bargaining and market processes and, in rejecting the Marxian model, Dahrendorf tends to underplay precisely these elements. Authority relations are much better understood if we recognise that, when Ego gives an order, Alter may well negotiate about what he is prepared to do, and the settlement may well be different from the original command. There is therefore some value in trying to extend the concepts of the market to cover cases of authority and obedience rather than the opposite, viz. subsuming all market relations under relations of authority.

However, from the point of view of our paradigm what we have to notice is this. In capitalist industrial organisations the major relationships are structured more or less overtly in terms of markets. Because of this they may also be understood as resting upon latent conflicts. But, just as we saw, the theory of markets could be extended to sacred areas, so also here we may say that if the theory of markets and of underlying power conflicts applies obviously to industrial organisations it may also usefully be extended to all other organisations whether or not they have economic purposes. Furthermore, market bargaining may be thought of as playing a part not merely in organisations in capitalist society but in Communist societies as well, even though the ideology of these latter societies denies the possibility. The value of Dahrendorf's work is that he suggests that the theory of conflict applies in this wider sphere. In authority relations and in relations arising from property, bargaining and market processes occur, and give rise to individual and collective bargaining and conflict.

6. *The collectivities involved in conflict*

Under the previous heading we drew attention to groups and organisations which could be thought of as coming into being as a result of market interaction, competition bargaining, conflict and a balance of power. The theory of conflict, however, also has to take account of groups which engage in conflict whether they exist prior to the conflict or come in to existence to pursue a conflict of goals or interests either directly or through the development of a market situation.

Nation states are the first point of reference here. They are compulsory political associations which can rely upon the loyalty of their members. They also exist within a world of states each of which has the right to use the ultimate sanction of violence on its own behalf. The limitations on this right to use violence are solely those which arise from the relatively undeveloped conventions and organisations governing international relations, the balance of power and the inherently dangerous quality of the means of violence themselves.

The process of international relations, however, is not simply a war of all against all or more exactly of each against each. States form alliances and some are simply the clients of others. They also form up in market systems where the individual participants are states rather than individuals with all the possibilities of equilibrium, disequilibrium and collective conflict which we outlined in the case of individuals.

The assertion of sovereignty by the state also takes place against other conflicting trends. The world economic order establishes bonds between individuals of different states and there are also cultural ties which unite individuals of different states. The existence of the state as a compulsory association therefore requires that these other spontaneously emerging bonds must be kept subordinate to the loyalty of the individual to his own state. Part of the sociological description of the international order, however, would include a description of these supra-national ties which compete with national loyalties.

Nations may exist without states, either because they have never achieved state sovereignty, or because they have lost it. Pure nationhood of this kind depends upon ties of kinship, common language and religion and a shared history and sense of place and community. Membership of a nation without a state is, however, difficult to sustain. It has to compete with a compulsory tie to the multi-national state within which it is subordinated and it may well be that loyalty to the intermediate nations will be difficult to sustain. What are normally given are the primordial ties of kinship, religion and community, and it could be that if these are tolerated no wider and more systematic drive to nationhood will develop. Individuals may be more or less committed to membership of the nation and the strength of the national group may depend upon the liveliness of its sense of a history of political conflict. Nationalism exists more strongly in the minds and hearts of 'extremists'. They face an everlasting problem of getting support amongst 'moderates'.

Rather different from the problem of nations without states and their relations with the states with sovereignty in which they are incorporated are the complex plural societies which came into being as the result of imperialism, conquest and colonial exploitation. Such groups may be bound together in the market-place, as Furnivall[11] suggests, or through political domination according to M. G. Smith.[12] They are, however, much stronger than the nations without states which we have been discussing, either because of their cultural differences or because of the fact of their separate history prior to and during the process of conquest. Plural society theory, of course, emphasises the degree to which, despite these differences, the various ethnic segments still constitute societies. The sociology of conflict places more emphasis upon difference, conflict and fissiparous tendencies.

There is a strong relationship between ethnic and national groupings in a political and economic order and social classes in the Marxian and Weberian sense. We may say that a national or ethnic group which is exploited by another national or ethnic group in the economic order has all the characteristics of the Marxian class-for-itself (and, of course, other characteristics besides). In most cases classes only approach the degree of cohesion to be found in a 'plural' ethnic segment. On the other hand it may be the case that class ties generated by the market and collective bargaining only partly coincide with the political and cultural ties of ethnic segments, even though for non-economic reasons these ties attract a powerful loyalty. In such cases Marxists will face a problem of 'false consciousness' amongst those whom they would expect to feel a primary class loyalty. In fact neither the primacy of ethnic or of class loyalty should be taken for granted. The actual state of play with regard to these competing loyalties will depend upon structural factors in the society itself.

Northern Ireland presents a good example of what we are talking about. Perhaps the primary fact of the situation is the exploitation and oppression of the Catholic working class by a bourgeoisie with foreign ties. None the less there are Protestant workers and Catholic employers, and part of the reason for the conflict is to be found in political as well as economic history. The exploited and oppressed in such a situation have to decide where both their class and national loyalties lie.

One cannot overemphasise the importance of the problems which we have just been discussing or their relative subordination in a Euro-centric sociology to the problematic of Marxism. The Northern Ireland case is only one of many. In the United States the structural problem of the relationships of Blacks to the economic and political order defies incorporation into a simple Marxian class analysis. So, too, does the case of the South African Black workers and peasants who, unlike the Blacks of the United States, are a majority. Most post-colonial states have a problem of ethnic pluralism. The struggle against colonialism and neo-colonialism has to face Fanon's[13] problem of the relative priority of national and socialist revolutions. Finally, in the advanced countries today we see the recruitment to the proletariat and sub-proletariat of a very considerable minority of 'ethnic' immigrant workers. No sociology today can claim to be complete which does not deal with these problems.

Yet with this said, the old Marxian problems remain. Whether or not there are ethnic divisions, class conflict is something which is generated in all advanced capitalist societies as an inevitable result of collective bargaining in the labour market. It may well also be argued that it is a process to be found in social-ist societies, whether through the continuation of labour market processes or through the operation of the more extended sort of class conflict between those with and without power.

The class-in-itself, class-for-itself problematic of Marxism helps us to formulate the structural problems here. Clearly, the simplest sort of group formation is that which occurs amongst groups seeking a monopoly in the market (e.g. trade unions and employers' organisations). Such groups, however, may move towards organising across the whole gamut of institutional con-texts and may sooner or later transcend the constraints placed upon their conflicts within the state, challenging even its mono-poly to the use of physical violence.

The task of the sociology of conflict in this area is to locate each case according to the range and the drasticness of the con-flict involved. On the other hand, it may also come to see any national social order not as a permanently smoothly functioning system but as occupying a particular empirical place within the range of ruling-class, truce and revolutionary situations.[14]

7. *Conflict, contradiction and social systems*

The concept of conflict as we have used it throughout this book has reference to meaningful action in pursuit of goals. The con-cept of contradiction has no such clear meaning. It is essentially a logical concept, which is especially popular with contemporary Marxism, because that Marxism has taken over the notion of the dialectic from Hegel. Of course, Marxists would claim that Marxism inverts the dialectic, but the 'sensuous human activ-ity'[15] which replaces thought in this inversion is still related to the concept of contradiction even though it is not clear what is meant by 'contradictory activity'.

It is of course possible to look at social structure in a thoroughly idealistic way as embodying certain 'principles' and to see such principles as possibly contradicting one another. Such an approach, however, does not achieve anything like the understanding which is achieved by looking at social relations as dependent upon action which is thought of as having subjective meaning. It is also quite inappropriate in a sociological system which calls itself materialist.

What may be meant by 'contradiction', however, is something different from this somewhat mystified usage. It may refer to a clash of goals which are pursued within different institutions. Perhaps the appropriate term to describe this is 'system-conflict'. This is a legitimate area of concern for the sociology of conflict and it is to this that we now turn.

Whether the number of participants in a system of social interaction is large or small it will be necessary, whatever other preferential ends the participants seek, that they should satisfy their basic survival needs and that the means should be provided for the continuation of the social framework within which they work. The early anthropological functionalism of Malinowski[16] suggested the kind of needs which had to be met. According to him, apart from basic biological needs, provision had to be made in a social system for distributing power, for applying norms for training new participants and for sustaining the material apparatus. One might argue with this as an exhaustive list of needs, but any sociology must surely have some such list.

In the earlier sections of this chapter we have in effect accepted the utilitarian assumption of the randomness of ends. This is a matter of convenience and it enables us to focus on certain kinds of problems. It is, however, the case that basic social structures within which conflict is pursued have to be sustained and the oversimplified models which we have used may well require elaboration to take account of this. We may also find that this elaboration is essential for the development of a macro-sociology of whole societies.

The central notions of conflict theory when applied to societies as systems of institutions are these:

1. Conflict may occur between actors in any of the institutional systems (i.e. there may be conflict between participants in industrial, political, religious and educational institutions);

2. Institutions are relatively dependent on one another so that one may expect that conflict in one institution will reflect conflict in another; in particular conflict in the basic institutions will be reflected in the secondary ones (e.g. where the conflict of interests in the labour market is reflected in ideological conflict);

3. It is also possible, however, since each institution 'takes on a

life of its own' that its purposes and internal conflicts of purpose may not be merely reflections of what goes on in other
institutions (thus religious conflict in particular societies may
come to have independence of or even dominance over industrial conflict). In this case there will be inter-institutional
conflict.

This type of problem has, of course, preoccupied recent
French Marxism.[17] Inheriting as it does the crude economic
functionalism of Plekhanov and Bukharin which posits basic
economic institutions which determine what goes on in the
'superstructure', it insists that these superstructural institutions
may be temporarily in dominance in a particular society. This
dominance, however, is something which is set up by the mode
of production which determines the pattern of the social formation 'in the last instance'.

However, before we can comment on this sophisticated comment on the problem of economic determinism we must ask
what is meant by the basic social institutions. For Malinowski
the basic institutions are those which satisfy biological needs.
For some Marxists they are the institutions of production. For
others they are economic institutions. There is also another tradition running through sociology and even through Marxism
which emphasises political conflict or power struggles as basic.

A central and often too little discussed problem here is the
meaning of 'economic'. Clearly, economic determinism differs
from the biological determinism of Malinowski. But does it
mean only that in the case of man it is not mere survival but
'production' which is his central concern? (A notion, inciden-
tally, which is clearly set out in the 104th Psalm, verse 23 where
in contrast to the animals, for whom nature makes provision, it
is said of man that he 'goeth forth unto his work, and to his
labour until the evening'.)

Production, however, is not necessarily organised on
'economic lines' (i.e. in terms of a series of markets). It may be
organised in terms of planned provision as in the oikos. On the
other hand the meeting of needs through the setting up of markets may become central to 'production', but may also be used
as a way of providing for other needs.

What then should be regarded as the basic institution: (a) in all societies; (b) in the advanced industrial countries? Clearly, it is the case that productive institutions are basic to all societies because there is no answer to the question, 'What happens to men who do not produce their own subsistence other than that they will die'? But it does also seem to be the case that in the last 400 years men have relied upon the market mechanism for ensuring that production occurs and it is therefore natural that a sociology should have arisen which treats the market as the basic institution and sees other institutions as having the function of maintaining the market order. It is surprising that modern Marxists, who devote such attention to studying the ways in which various other institutions have been set up in dominance in pre-capitalist societies, should not have noticed that what happens in capitalist industrial society is that although production may be the determining influence in the last instance it is the market system which is in dominance. It may even be the case that it plays a very large part in post-capitalist and socialist societies.

The thrust of our own argument in this book is certainly to suggest that market systems and their breakdown into conflict are quite central to the development of the advanced societies. We have also suggested, however, that there may be other kinds of conflicts, both external between nation states and internal to nation states, which may be unrelated to or only partially related to conflicts generated by the market. We suggest that a comprehensive sociology should, while recognising the truth that without production men die, and while giving due weight to market processes, be prepared to treat all of these major political conflicts as basic.

Given the recognition that the basic institutions of an advanced and complex society express these political conflicts, we may then turn to the so-called secondary institutions. One would expect say religion and education in England to reflect its market-class and status conflicts. One would expect these institutions in Ireland to reflect the fact that Catholics and Protestants are more or less at war. In South Africa one would expect all institutions to reflect the fact of race and class struggle. On the other hand one might expect what some call 'contradiction' or what we would call 'inter-institutional conflict' when secondary institutions take on a life of their own or when they reflect tendencies within a wide international order.

The aim of this chapter has not, of course, been to give an account of what the social world is like. Its aim has been to indicate the areas in which a sociologist, guided by conflict theory, would feel equipped to undertake investigations given the problematic from which he starts. It is in the nature of that problematic that it does not start as functionalism does with a single whole called 'society' or 'the social system' and then look at its functioning parts. Rather if focuses on any kind of social interaction within which conflict may occur and, starting from this centre, works its way out as far as possible systematically to look at consequent problems.

A working paradigm for conflict sociology

For purposes of convenience and in order to indicate the major differences between the sociology of conflict as a general sociological theory, we suggest the following 'paradigm' for conflict analysis which may be contrasted with Merton's 'Paradigm for functional analysis'[18] or Parsons' 'Paradigm of the action elements'.[19]

Paradigm for Conflict Analysis

I Basic processes to be brought into focus
(*a*) Dyadic conflict.
    (i) Between individuals:
        (a) purely rational calculating conflict;
        (b) conflict involving affective interaction.
    (ii) Between collectivities.

In all of these conflicts variables include the effectiveness of communication between parties, the degree to which they are responsive to normative and effective constraints, and their capacity to mobilise sanctions in support of their own demands.

Conflict situations may lead after the deployment of sanctions to the maintenance of the status quo, to truce and compromise or to 'revolution'. Many situations treated in functionalist theory as based upon a consensus about norms turn out on analysis to rest upon domination or upon a truce in a power struggle.

(*b*) Bargaining and the market.
  (i) Exchanges which are mutually beneficial and which maximise the utility of both or all parties.
  (ii) Exchanges which have the qualities mentioned in (*a*) but which are beneficial only on the assumption that the existing distribution of property is not to be disturbed.
  (iii) Free market situations in which the sanction 'going to another supplier' is available and in which, out of the process of competition and bargaining, the highest degree of individual satisfaction possible is attained.
  (iv) Situations as above but which are beneficial to individuals only on the assumption that the existing distribution of property is not to be disturbed.
  (v) Oligopolistic and monopolistic situations leading to collective bargaining and power conflict:
    (a) subject to normative regulation and limitation on the use of drastic sanctions;
    (b) involving no limit to sanctions used with breakdown of law and order.

The development of market negotiation to the point indicated under (b)(v)(ii) involves the transcendence of purely economic conflict and its translation to the political sphere. Here one would have Marx's classes-for-themselves and functionally related conflicts 'across the board'.

II. Groups structured through market processes
(*a*) The structure of the industrial firm understood as a series of negotiated truces after collective bargaining in markets for capital, raw materials, labour and customers.
(*b*) Structures of command in industry and elsewhere understood as resulting from market-like negotiations.
(*c*) Incipient class conflict in situations II(*a*) and II(*b*) and the mechanisms for containing and institutionalising it.

III. Collectivities in conflict
(*a*) The world of nation states governed by only limited conventions and organisations.
  (i) Alliances and clientage.
  (ii) Super-power conflict.
  (iii) Conflict between medium and small powers.
(*b*) Nations without states.
  (i) Quiescent ethnic minorities.
  (ii) Mobilised ethnic minorities:
    (a) the nature of primordial ties, e.g. kinship, language, religion;
    (b) awareness of conflict with incorporating state;
    (c) strategies for exacerbating conflict and facilitating mobilisation.

(*c*) Plural societies.
  (i) Processes of constructing multi-ethnic colonial states:
    (a) economic exploitation;
    (b) political conquest and domination.
  (ii) Relationship of ethnicity and class.
  (iii) Post-colonial and neo-colonial processes:
    (a) the internal allies of the neo-colonial power;
    (b) division of labour and power between ethnic minorities;
    (c) conflict, balance of power and merging of ethnicities.

IV. Conflict and social systems
(*a*) Problem of the basic institution.
   Relative role of biological institutions.
   Institutions of production.
   The market.
   Basic political conflicts.
(*b*) The reflection of conflicts in secondary institutions and structures.
(*c*) Conflicts of purpose engendered by relative independence of institutions.

Here at least is a starting point for a general and systematic approach to sociology in a world which is far from conforming to the polar type outlined in Parsons' *Social System*. It is also at odds with the more flexible use of functionalist theory suggested by Merton. Neither of these ultimately puts conflict at the centre of theory. The paradigm suggested here is, it is claimed, a more inclusive one than that of functionalism, interpreting the social order which it perceives as the outcome of balances of power and truces.

REFERENCES AND FURTHER READING

Chapter 1 The micro-sociology of conflict

1. Talcott Parsons, *The Social System*, Tavistock, London, 1952.
2. Ibid., p. 39.
3. Talcott Parsons, *The Structure of Social Action*, Free Press, Glencoe, Illinois, 1949 (see especially pp. 77–81), and Talcott Parsons and Edward Shils eds, *Toward a General Theory of Action*, Harvard University Press, Cambridge, Mass., 1952.
4. Karl Popper, *The Poverty of Historicism*, Routledge and Kegan Paul, London, 1957, p. 136.
5. Max Weber, *Economy and Society*, Vol. 1, Bedminster Press, New York 1968, p. 13.
6. Ibid., p. 9.
7. Ibid., p. 9.
8. Ibid., p. 38.
9. Emile Durkheim, *The Rules of Sociological Method*, Free Press, Glencoe, Illinois, 1938.
10. For a lucid discussion of these issues from a structuralist point of view, see Anthony Giddens, *Central Problems of Social Theory*, MacMillan, London, 1979. Giddens, however, devotes little space to the discussion of the alternative tradition of methodological individualism.
11. Parsons, *Social System*, p. 38.
12. Parsons, *Structure of Social Action*, pp. 77–81.
13. Parsons, *Social System*, Ch. VII.
14. David Matza, *Delinquency and Drift*, Wiley, New York, 1964.
15. Jurgen Habermas, *Legitimation Crisis*, Heinemann, London, 1976.
16. Neil Smelser, *The Theory of Collective Behaviour*, Routledge and Kegan Paul, London, 1962.
17. See especially Harold Garfinkel, *Studies in Ethnomethodology*, Prentice-Hall, New Jersey, 1967.
18. Weber, op. cit., p. 212.
19. Amitai Etzioni, *The Active Society*, Free Press, New York, 1968, p. 96.
20. Parsons, *Structure of Social Action*, Chs. 8 and 9, especially pp. 378–90.
21. Parsons, *Social System*, Ch. 6.
22. Weber, op. cit., Ch. 3.
23. Robert Merton, 'Social structure and anomie' in *Social Theory and Social Structure*, Free Press, New York, 1957.

24. Parsons, *Social System* and Parsons and Shils (eds), *Toward a General Theory of Action*.
25. Whether it is more than simply a myth is discussed in a most interesting section of Habermas' *Legitimation Crisis* (see pp. 95. 162). Habermas, intent on maintaining the unity between scientific and moral discourse, suggests that Weber's analysis of rational–legal authority as an empirical fact in Western civilisation goes right to the boundaries of these two types of discourse without ever crossing them.
26. Karl Mannheim, *Ideology and Utopia*, Routledge and Kegan Paul, London, 1954.
27. See Ian Taylor, Paul Walton and Jock Young, *The New Criminology*, Routledge and Kegan Paul, London, 1974.
28. At a conference in Ghana on Positive Action for Peace and Security in Africa attended by the author in 1960.
29. See Talcott Parsons, *Structure and Process in Modern Societies*, Free Press, New York 1964, Ch. 6.
30. William Graham Sumner, *Folkways*, Ginn and Co., Boston, 1907.
31. Emile Durkheim, *The Elementary Forms of Religious Life*, Allen and Unwin, London, 1915, p. 207.
32. George Herbert Mead, *Mind Self and Society*, University of Chicago, Chicago, 1967.
33. Weber, op. cit, Ch. 3.
34. Parsons, *Social System*, Ch. 7.
35. Merton, op. cit.
36. Parsons, *Social System*, p. 258.

Chapter 2 Conflict and market situations

1. For an overview of Simmel's major contributions to general sociological theory see Kurt Wolff ed., *The Sociology of Georg Simmel*, Free Press, New York 1950 and Kurt Wolff (ed.), *Georg Simmel 1858–1958*, Ohio State University, Columbus, Ohio, 1959. The latter volume contains an excellent bibliography.
2. See Georg Simmel, *Conflict and the Web of Group Affiliations* (with a foreword by Everett C. Hughes) and Lewis Coser, *The Functions of Social Conflict*, Routledge and Kegan Paul, London, 1956.
3. Georg Simmel, *The Philosophy of Money*, Routledge and Kegan Paul, London, 1978.
4. Bronislav Malinowski, *Crime and Custom in Savage Society*, Routledge and Kegan Paul, London, 1926.
5. Peter Blau, *Exchange and Power in Social Life*, Wiley, New York, 1967.
6. Henry Sumner Maine, *Ancient Law*, Henry Holt, New York, 1906.
7. Herbert Spencer, *Principles of Sociology*, Williams and Norgate, London, 1897–1906. See especially the chapter on industrial society.
8. Bronislav Malinowski, *Argonauts of the Western Pacific*, Routledge and Kegan Paul, London, 1922, and *Coral Gardens and their Magic*, American Book Co., New York, 1935.
9. See Malinowski, *Crime and Custom in Savage Society*.
10. See Franz Boas, *The Social Organisation and Secret Societies of the Kwakiutl Indians*, Report of the US National Museum, 1895.

11. See Raymond Firth, *Human Types*, Mentor Books, 1958, and *Primitive Economics of the New Zealand Maori*, Dutton, New York, 1929.
12. Benjamin Nelson, *The Idea of Usury – From Tribal Brotherhood to Universal Otherhood*, University of Chicago Press, Chicago, 1969.
13. Talcott Parsons, *The Structure of Social Action*, Free Press, New York, 1937, and Emile Durkheim, *The Division of Labour in Society*, Macmillan, New York, 1933.
14. Max Weber, *Economy and Society*, Vol. 2, Bedminster Press, New York, 1968, p. 927.
15. Ibid., pp. 927–8.
16. According to the industrial lawyer Kahn-Freund: 'Reliance on legislation and legal sanctions for the enforcement of rights and duties between employers and employees may be a sign of impending breakdown and, especially on the side of the unions, frequently a sign of weakness, certainly not a sign of strength' in H.A. Clegg, and A Flanders, *The System of Industrial Relations in Great Britain*, Basil Blackwell, Oxford, 1954, p. 44.
17. John Rex, *Key Problems of Sociological Theory*, Routledge and Kegan Paul, London, 1961.
18. For an interesting discussion of Lenin's views on this question, see Merle Fainsod, *How Russia is Ruled*, Harvard University Press, Cambridge, Mass., 1956.
19. Max Black, (ed.) *The Social Theories of Talcott Parsons*, Prentice-Hall, New Jersey, 1961, p. 33.
20. Durkheim, op. cit.
21. Weber, op. cit., Vol. 1, pp. 85–6.
22. Karl Marx, *Economic and Philosophical Manuscripts of 1844*, in Marx-Engels, *Selected Works*, Vol. 3, Foreign Languages Publishing House, Moscow, 1975, p. 273.
23. Milovan Djilas, *The New Class*, Praeger, New York, 1957.
24. John Rex, and Robert Moore, *Race, Community and Conflict*, Oxford University Press, London, 1967.
25. Colin Bell, 'On housing classes', *Australian and New Zealand Journal of Sociology*, **13**, No. 1, February 1977.
26. Karl Marx, *The Poverty of Philosophy*, in Marx-Engels, *Selected Works*, Vol. 4, Foreign Languages Publishing House, Moscow, 1976.

Chapter 3 Conflict and social systems

1. David Lockwood, 'Social integration and systems integration' in George Zollschan and Walter Hirsch, *Explorations in Social Change*, Routledge and Kegan Paul, London, 1964.
2. For a discussion of neo-Marxist and structuralist usages of the concept of contradiction see Anthony Giddens, *Central Problems in Social Theory*, Macmillan, London, 1979, Ch. 4.
3. See Ludwig Von Bertalanffy, 'General systems theory' in N. J. Demerath III, and Richard A. Paterson, *Systems Change and Conflict*, Free Press, New York, 1967.
4. See Talcott Parsons, *The Structure of Social Action*, Free Press, New York, 1937, and L. J. Henderson, *Pareto's General Sociology: A Physiologist's Interpretation*. Harvard University Press, Cambridge, Mass., 1935.

5. This change dated from Parsons' collaborative work with Bales. See Talcott Parsons, Robert Bales and Edward Shils, *Working Papers on the Theory of Action*, Free Press, New York 1953, and Talcott Parsons and Neil Smelser, *Economy and Society*, Routledge and Kegan Paul, London, 1956.

6. Parsons, *Structure of Social Action*, p. 181.

7. The key works here were Bronislav Malinowski, *A Scientific Theory of Culture*, University of North Carolina Press, Chapel Hill, 1944; Alfred Reginald Radcliffe-Brown, *Structure and Function in Primitive Societies*, Cohen and West, London, 1968; and Robert Merton, 'Manifest and latent functions' in *Social Theory and Social Structure*, Free Press, New York, 1957.

8. This involves a deduction from Weber's concepts of closed social relationships and of the imputation of responsibility. See Max Weber, *Economy and Society*, Vol. 1, Bedminster Press, New York, 1968, Ch. 1. See also John Rex, *Sociology and the Demystification of the Modern World*, Routledge and Kegan Paul, 1974, p. 78.

9. Ferdinand Tonnies, *Community and Association*, translated and supplemented by Charles P. Loomis, Routledge and Kegan Paul, London, 1955.

10. Robert MacIver and Charles Page, *Society – An Introductory Analysis*, Macmillan, London, 1950.

11. David Lockwood, 'Some remarks on "The Social System"', *British Journal of Sociology*, 7, June 1956. Also Zollschan and Hirsch, op. cit.

12. Talcott Parsons, 'Malinowski and the theory of social systems' in Raymond Firth, *Man and Culture*, Routledge and Kegan Paul, London, 1957.

13. Malinowski, op. cit., pp. 163–7 deal specifically with the bases of group formation.

14. Merton, op. cit.

15. Parsons, *Structure of Social Action*, p. 77.

16. Richard Niebuhr, *The Social Sources of Denominationalism*, Holt, New York, 1929.

17. Weber, op. cit., Vol. 2. pp. 932–7.

18. Lockwood, in Zollschan and Hirsch, op. cit.

19. Radcliffe-Brown, op. cit.

20. Merton, op. cit., p. 74.

21. Ibid., p. 52.

22. Karl Marx, *Preface to a Contribution to the Critique of Political Economy* in Marx-Engels, *Selected Works*, Vol. 1, Foreign Languages Publishing House; Moscow, 1951.

23. Karl Marx, *Theses on Feuerbach* in Marx-Engels, *On Religion*, Foreign Languages Publishing House, Moscow, 1957.

24. See the various writings of Louis Althusser, e.g. Louis Althusser, *For Marx*, Allen Lane, London, 1969; Louis Althusser and Etienne Balibar, *Reading Capital*, New Left Books, London, 1970; Louis Althusser, *Lenin and Philosophy and Other Essays*, New Left Books, London, 1971.

25. Althusser, *For Marx*.

26. Sol Piciotto, and John Holloway, *State and Capital: A Marxist Debate*, Edward Arnold, London, 1977.

27. See especially Lewis A. Coser, *The Functions of Social Conflict*, Free Press, New York, 1956.

28. It is of some interest that the account of an utterly despotic society given by Karl Wittfogel in his *Oriental Despotism*, Yale University, New Haven and London, 1957, fits entirely with the theory of cross-cutting conflicts.

29. See especially Neil Smelser, *The Theory of Collective Behaviour*, Routledge and Kegan Paul, London, 1962, and William Kornhauser, *The Politics of Mass Society*, Routledge and Kegan Paul, London, 1960.

30. Max Gluckman, *Custom and Conflict in Africa*, Basil Blackwell, London, 1955.

Chapter 4 Collectivities in conflict

1. We are assuming here Max Weber's definition of the state as 'a compulsory political organisation' whose 'administrative staff successfully uphold the claim to the monopoly of the legitimate use of physical force in the enforcement of its order'. Economy and Society, Vol. 1, Bedminster Press, New York, 1967, Ch. 1, p. 54.

2. See Milton J. Esman, *Ethnic Conflict in the Western World*, Cornell University Press, Ithaca, 1977.

3. See Alvin Gouldner, *The Dialectic of Ideology and Technology*, Macmillan, London, 1976, p. 24.

4. J. S. Furnivall, *Netherlands India*, Cambridge University Press, Cambridge, 1967.

5. M. G. Smith, *The Plural Society in the British West Indies*, University of California Press, Berkeley and Los Angeles, 1965.

6. John Rex, 'The plural society in sociological theory', *British Journal of Sociology*, X No. 2, June 1959.

7. See especially *Contribution to the Critique of Hegel's Philosophy of Right* in Robert Tucker, *The Marx-Engels Reader*, W. W. Norson and Co., New York, 1972. The significance of this work is discussed from different perspectives in Robert Tucker, *Philosophy and Myth in Karl Marx*, Cambridge University Press London 1965, and Shlomo Avineri, *The Social and Political Thought of Karl Marx*, Oxford University Press, London, 1964.

8. Richard Hoggart, *The Uses of Literacy*, Penguin Books, Harmondsworth, 1958.

9. Karl Marx, 'Contribution to the Critique of Hegel's Philosophy of Right'.

10 John Rex, *Key Problems of Sociological Theory*, Routledge and Kegan Paul, London, 1961.

11. Ferdinand Tönnies, *Gemeinschaft und Gesellschaft*, translated as *Community and Association* by C. P. Loomis, Routledge and Kegan Paul, London, 1955.

12. Franz Oppenheimer, *The State*, Ind, Vanguard Press, New York, 1926.

13. Karl Marx, and Frederick Engels, *The Communist Manifesto* in Marx-Engels, *Selected Works*, Vol. 1, Foreign Languages Publishing House, Moscow, 1951.

14. Richard Niebuhr, *The Social Sources of Denominationalism*, Meridian Books, New York, 1975.

15. Ralf Dahrendorf, *Class and Class Conflict in Industrial Societies*, Routledge and Kegan Paul, London 1959.

16. James Burnham, *The Managerial Revolution*, Penguin Books, Harmondsworth, 1945.

17. See Merle Fainsod, *How Russia is Ruled*, Harvard University Press, Cambridge, Mass., 1956.

18. See Frank Parkin, *Marxism and Class Theory – A Bourgeois Critique*, Tavistock, London, 1979.

19. Gunnar Myrdal, *Challenge to Affluence*, Gollancz, London, 1964.
20. John Rex and Sally Tomlinson, *Colonial Immigrants in a British City*, Routledge and Kegan Paul, London, 1979.

Chapter 5 A paradigm for conflict analysis

1. Talcott Parsons, *Structure and Process in Modern Societies*, Free Press, New York, 1960, Ch. VI.
2. See Parsons' Introduction to Max Weber, *The Theory of Social and Economic Organisation*, Oxford University Press, London, 1947.
3. See Talcott Parsons, *The Social System*, Tavistock, London, 1952, Chs. 6–8.
4. Ibid., Ch. 8.
5. See for instance Eric Fromm, *The Fear of Freedom*, Routledge and Kegan Paul, London, 1957.
6. Kurt Wolff, *The Sociology of Georg Simmel*, Pt. 2, Free Press, New York 1950, Ch. 3.
7. Ibid., Pt. 2, Ch. 5 and Pt. 5, Ch. 4.
8. Max Weber, *Economy and Society*, Vol. 1, Bedminster Press, New York, 1967, Ch. 2.
9. Ibid., Ch. 9, Sect. 6.
10. Ralf Dahrendorf, *Class and Class Conflict in Industrial Societies*, Routledge and Kegan Paul, London, 1959.
11. J. R. Furnivall, *Netherlands India*, Cambridge University Press, Cambridge, 1967.
12. M. G. Smith, *The Plural Society in the British West Indies*, University of California Press, Berkeley, 1965.
13. Frantz Fanon, *The Wretched of the Earth*, Penguin Books, Harmondsworth, 1967.
14. John Rex, *Key Problems of Sociological Theory*, Routledge and Kegan Paul, London, 1961.
15. *Theses on Feuerbach* in *Marx-Engels Collected Works*, Moscow Foreign Languages Publishing House, Moscow. See especially the First Thesis.
16. Bronislav Malinowski; *A Scientific Theory of Culture*, University of North Carolina Press, Chapel Hill, 1944.
17. See Louis Althusser, *For Marx*, Allen Lane, London 1969, and *Lenin and Philosophy* New Left Books, London, 1971.
18. Robert Merton, *Social Theory and Social Structure*, Free Press, New York, 1964, p. 50.
19. Talcott Parsons, *Social System*, p. 57.

INDEX